Table of Contents

Dark Psychology 101 2021:
Understanding the Techniques of Covert Manipulation, Mind Control, Influence, and Persuasion

Introduction 2
Chapter 1: What Is Dark Psychology? 7
Chapter 2: How Prevalent Is Dark Psychology? 18
Chapter 3: How Do I Recognize When Dark Psychology Is Being Used? 30
Chapter 4: Manipulation Techniques 42
   Persuasion 43
   Taking Over a Room/Becoming "Alpha" 47
   Online Grooming 56
Chapter 5: What Is Mind Control? 59
   Hypnosis 59
   Gaslighting 61
   Cults 68
Chapter 6: Dark Psychology and Seduction 70
Chapter 7: The Dark Triad 79
   Sociopath 80
   Narcissist 82
   Machiavellian 84
   Dark Psychology Tactics of the Dark Triad 85
Chapter 8: The Art of Deception and Mind Games 90
   Cold Reading 98
Chapter 9: What Is Brainwashing? 101
Chapter 10: The Importance of Body Language 106
   Dominance 107
   Seduction 110
   Interest vs. Boredom 113
Chapter 11: Best Practices and Defenses 116
   Trust Is a Commodity to Be Earned—Not Freely Given 116

Don't Drink Alone 117
Don't Be Afraid to Disengage 117
Have a Panic Button 118
Call Them Out 118
Continue Your Study and Research of Dark Psychology Tactics 119
Spread the Word 119

Conclusion 122

Dark Psychology Secrets 2021:
Defenses Against Covert Manipulation, Mind Control, NLP, Emotional Influence, Deception, and Brainwashing

Introduction 126

Chapter 1: The Art of Manipulation 132
Goals and Intents of Manipulation 133
Where Is Manipulation Used? 136
Who Uses Manipulation and Dark Psychology? 136
Why Is Learning About Manipulation Important? 138

Chapter 2: The Importance of Reading People 141
Reading People From a Dark Psychology User's 141
Reading People From a Potential Victim's Point of View 145

Chapter 3: Manipulation Techniques 149
Three Modes of Persuasion 149
Emotional Manipulation 152
Power Play and Dominance 155
Charm and Flattery/Mirroring 157

Chapter 4: Emotional Manipulation 161
Short-Term Manipulation 161
Long-Term Manipulation 163

Chapter 5: The Importance of Self-Esteem 168
The "Ideal Woman" 168
Build Self-Esteem Through Meditation 171
Take Care of Your Health and Body 173
Build a Support System 173

Chapter 6: Workplace Manipulation 177
  Using Manipulation to Climb the Corporate Ladder.................... 177
  Using Manipulation to Defend One's Position 178
  Using Manipulation to Gain Power Over Colleagues.................... 182

Chapter 7: Manipulative Partners 186
  Flattery and Superficial Charm.................... 187
  Gradual Emotional Breakdown 189
  Attachment and the Fear of Loss 191

Chapter 8: Acceptable Influence vs. Toxic Manipulation.................... 195
  Tolerable Manipulation and Influence 196
  Not All Intentions Are Malicious 200

Chapter 9: Manipulative Family Members.................... 202
  The Child as the Manipulator 202
  The Parent as the Manipulator 206

Chapter 10: Defenses Against Brainwashing.................... 211
  How Is Brainwashing Accomplished? 211
  How to Avoid Brainwashing? 217

Chapter 11: Neuro-Linguistic Programming.................... 220
  What Is NLP?.................... 220
  How is NLP Used in a Manipulation Scheme? 225

Chapter 12: Covert Mind Control 229
  The Subliminal Message Experiment 229
  Art of Embedded Commands 231
  How to Protect Yourself From Covert Mind Control.................... 236

Chapter 13: Recognizing Manipulators 238
  They Constantly Challenge You to Prove Yourself.................... 238
  They Are Passive-Aggressive.................... 239
  They Use Gaslighting on You 239
  They Use Humor as a Weapon Against You 240
  They Are Always the Victim 240
  They Use Kindness as a Weapon 240
  They Belittle Your Pain 241

   They Keep Their Cool to Magnify Your Own Emotions 241
Chapter 14: Manipulating Manipulators 242
   Mirror the Manipulator 242
   Be Immune to the Manipulator's Charms 243
   Be Aware of Your Emotions 244
Conclusion 246

Dark Psychology 101 2021:

Understanding the Techniques of Covert Manipulation, Mind Control, Influence, and Persuasion

Introduction

Congratulations on purchasing *Dark Psychology 101 2021*, and thank you for doing so.

The following chapters will discuss all the major topics related to dark psychology. You will first learn about the key concepts and definitions involved  when we talk about dark psychology before jumping into specific techniques, tools, and strategies used by many different types of people worldwide. The people who practice dark psychology are as varied and unique as the strategies themselves. While some practitioners spend hours, days, or years of their lives studying the psychology behind these practices, some people develop a natural "talent" for things like manipulation and mind games because they've learned that people can be easy prey once they realize the commonalities of human psychology and how to exploit the more influential aspects of the human character and traits like empathy, sociability, kindness, and gullibility. These traits would be considered positive and signals of a good person in a normal working society. Think of the young girl on her way to school who is everyone's friend and offers her time to charity and extracurricular work. The person who offers help to complete strangers when they ask for it has not experienced the darker sides of humanity.

But for the manipulator, these personality traits don't just signal someone who might give them a helping hand in whatever situation. They see someone they can use to their advantage through dark psychology techniques and practices. We call these people predators, criminals, and scam artists; the list goes on. So while a kind, trusting person is a great thing, there is still the reality to acknowledge that there are less favorable people out there constantly on the lookout for personalities that can be easily manipulated.

In this book, you'll be introduced to what exactly dark psychology is and how to recognize it. You'll learn how important it is to be aware when these strategies may be used on you or someone you know or care about. In chapter 2, we'll discuss the startling prevalence of practitioners of dark psychology, as well as where these people are often found in modern day society. Where do they operate? What do they look for? How successful are they in different arenas?

In the next chapter, you'll learn how to recognize when someone is using dark psychology techniques on you and how to spot it when it's happening, as well as how to derail the person's efforts before they get something from you that you didn't even know you were offering. These lessons can be life-saving, so pay attention to the tips and tricks in this chapter.

In chapter 4, we'll talk about some specific techniques used in manipulation by looking at a few examples of these practitioners in action. You'll learn specific terminology used to refer to these techniques, and we will illustrate a complete scene where those strategies may be used. In all likelihood, you've been present in a situation in which someone was trying to manipulate someone nearby. Public places like bars and even coffee shops can be a hunting ground for those looking for the perfect opportunity to "meet" someone new to prime them for manipulation.

In the next chapter, we'll discuss mind control in particular. We'll define terms and tools like gaslighting and discuss how incredibly damaging these experiences can be for victims.

Chapter 6 is all about how dark psychology is used specifically to seduce and gain the trust of someone they hope to exploit sexually or emotionally. There are many different angles and degrees to which these practices are applied and practiced. We are talking about both the young man who lies and showers compliments to get a girl to come home with him, as well as the latest serial killer looking to gain the affection or pity of a naïve girl just long enough to get her in his car.

The Dark Triad is the topic of chapter 7, which includes the three-pronged collection of personalities that are most often associated with the practice of dark psychology. They are the narcissist, the sociopath, and the Machiavellian personality types. You will learn what differentiates these three types, as well as how they are similar. By the end of this chapter, you will have learned several tips on how to spot someone who falls into one of these categories.

In chapter 8, we'll discuss the art of deception and the mind games that often accompany them. Deception is a broad term and includes such innocent practices as a magician using sleight of hand to convince an audience that something is happening when it really isn't. It extends to the tricky tactics used by false mystics and mediums in a time when Harry Houdini traveled all over the place to catch these scam artists in the act as they tricked grieving widows out of their money.

We'll move on then to discuss the specifics of brainwashing, how it is done, who is vulnerable, and how to shut it down if you think someone is trying to use this technique on you or someone you know.

In chapter 10, we'll switch gears to discuss the importance of body language and how we all communicate using nonverbal communication. We will discuss micro-expressions and how to read another person or get them to like you quickly. These techniques are used by people all over the world. Some of these practitioners include people trying to climb the ladder at work by getting "in" with their superiors.

Finally, in chapter 11, we'll focus on best practices for defense against practitioners who routinely put these dark psychology strategies into practice. You've likely been a target in your lifetime, even if you have no idea what was going on. Perhaps the person was unsuccessful, or perhaps they were, but you didn't realize what had happened until it's too late. Some of you may be reading this book precisely because you have been a victim in the past, and you want to learn to protect yourself and recognize it when someone tries these tools on you again. Whatever your reason is for reading Dark Psychology, by the end of chapter 11, you will have given yourself some very important lessons regarding self-preservation and defense against the dark psychology arsenal.

There are plenty of books on this subject on the market, so thanks again for choosing this one! Every effort was made to ensure it is full of as much useful information as possible. Please enjoy!

Chapter 1: What Is Dark Psychology?

Dark Psychology is at once a simple and quite complex topic. It encompasses the ways in which one person gets something from another person without them being aware of their tactics or the motivation behind those tactics. Many practitioners become quite skilled at hiding ulterior motives. They put on a mask that conveys to people that their feelings or intent is straightforward when, in fact, they are anything but.

This is why we call the subject of dark psychology. The victim of dark psychology is most likely in the dark about what is happening to them, and the victim may never find out, or they may only figure things out when it is too late, or the perpetrator has moved on. Now, it is important to note that not all forms of dark psychology are inherently malicious. As mentioned in the introduction to this book, dark psychology includes things like sleight of hand in a magic show, which is used to entertain an audience. However, a skilled pickpocket can also use sleight of hand who roams around crowded tourist areas, stealing money and other easily accessible items. The key distinction is that the person on whom these practices are being applied does not know that this particular strategy is being used. As viewers, we may know that a magician is simply using a trick to convince us that something has disappeared, but we don't necessarily know the mechanism of that trick, even when we realize that we were fooled. Again, this is a lighthearted and entertaining application of dark psychology, but the kind we'll be discussing in this book is on the much darker and more malicious side of the spectrum.

Why is it important to learn about dark psychology? People decide to educate themselves on the strategies and tools of dark psychology for different reasons. Some may actually like to learn a few tricks of the trade in order to get ahead in some aspect of their lives, while others want to learn how to detect predators and steer clear of those who might seek to manipulate them. Whatever your reasons for picking up this book, you will indeed find that you are much more educated and prepared to engage with the concepts of dark psychology once you've completed this reading.

The only way to constructively discuss the origins of dark psychology is to discuss each topic individually. This is because, as stated earlier, dark psychology covers a vast amount of territory. It is certain that the most elementary and instinctive forms have existed in human society since organized society itself has been in existence. People rose to the top of the food chain and, over time, developed a system for recognizing the leaders or alphas to whom others would submit. This primitive hierarchy is still followed today in many social circles. For example, the group of high school boys who like to hang out at the mall might have one person in their group who is the most good-looking, the most athletic, the most charismatic, or even all three at once. When the group notices an attractive young girl, there is often an unspoken understanding that the alpha, or leader, gets first dibs. This is because no one else in the group is willing or capable of fighting the alpha with the intent to take his place. These things work almost without our active consciousness as a natural way to organize and make sense of ourselves as organizations of society. The same kind of thing happens at work, in school, in political office, etc.

Dark psychology comes into play in these areas of elementary social hierarchy when individuals use covert or manipulative behaviors in order to establish themselves higher up in that hierarchy. They may lie, cheat, or steal in order to establish their dominance and capability. Again, these behaviors are as old as human organized society itself, and their applications and variances are too numerable to count.

However, dark psychology has also integrated several different areas of specialization and research, which have been established and pursued to understand human behavior, psychology, and, finally, criminality. We know that human beings do not always interact with each other in totally benevolent ways, and the deviant human beings in our society are the ones causing the most harm and damage. Some researchers come to the discipline out of sheer interest and fascination, while other entities, like law enforcement, are obsessed with figuring out exactly what makes someone like the narcissistic serial killer tick. If they can unlock what is going on in these criminals' minds and understand their tactics, it would give them a leg up on their investigations. The problem is, as the very nature of these tactics is "dark," it is very difficult to detect the workings of  a criminal narcissist of sociopath until the damage is done and the victims come forward or, in the worst cases, bodies are recovered.

And, dark psychology does not solely exist in the realm of criminals. Especially in recent years, illegal and coercive interrogation tactics have come to light through major news outlets, documentaries, new evidence, and TV shows, which highlight the reality that sometimes, even the "good guys" will go to desperate measures to get what they want or maintain the reputations of their law enforcement organizations. False confessions leading to years or even life in prison are utilized in court and are sometimes proven false once the real culprits are caught. But sometimes, the guilty get away with their crimes when the incorrect person is blamed and convicted. Unfortunately, many of these cases reflect flagrant racism and laziness on the part of a few law enforcement officials. And, while there are thousands of skilled, honest officers and investigators working in modern society, extreme cases lead to grossly negative outcomes, which always make the front page.

The sensationalism and true crime popularity frenzy are partially to blame for a reignited interest in dark psychology by those who do not work in realms like law enforcement. Now, it feels increasingly important to be able to defend and rely on yourself in these situations where dark psychology is used maliciously. It may be statistically unlikely that you are going to come face to face with a manipulative serial killer or a sociopathic, gaslighting boyfriend, but you certainly would want to have been prepared in the case where you hit on that narrow likelihood, wouldn't you?

This is why I can't say that reporting, social media, a renewed interest in true crime, corruption in the law enforcement arena, and dark psychology are altogether unfortunate evolution in the age of personal responsibility. As our cities get bigger and political and social unrest grow in intensity, the hunting

grounds ripe with potential targets become larger and closer together. There is no downside to taking it upon yourself to become educated and more aware of the potential threats in modern society.

With that said, there is another facet to dark psychology that we will explore that has a lot more to do with active observation and positive psychology and a lot less to do with serial killers.

Neuro-linguistic programming and other facets of psychology research focus on reprogramming your brain to perform better or differently as a way to relieve negative disorders that affect people's lives, such as depression and anxiety. NLP, in particular, is used in many situations by people who seek to teach their brains to reinterpret those triggers which have always prompted negative feelings. These harmful mental experiences can often lead to lifelong struggles of becoming productive and fulfilled. And this may lead to isolation, loneliness, perceived failures, and often, a deepening of those underlying mood disorders. NLP is one way to help a person retrain their brains in those moments when it really counts. This strategy, developed in the 70s, utilizes the brain's relationship to language and how it interprets language and information in everyday life. It teaches the brain through repetition and consistent application to replace those feelings of anxiety, fear, self-doubt, etc., with more positive and constructive emotional and behavioral reactions. The research and application of NLP have improved many people's lives, and, in particular, it has been useful in treating those mental states which arise from a particular trauma or past experience with an emotional manipulator.

The Dark Triad personalities date back much further and encompass the realm of the narcissist, the sociopath, and the Machiavellian types. While these personalities themselves have existed in human beings for probably as long as we've been organizing into societies, the actual focus on research and understanding in terms of psychology is much more recent. It was recognized that it is not just important to be able to identify these individuals in society. We also need to have some basis of understanding in order to combat and prevent the potential harm inflicted on these people's targets.

While many forms of dark psychology can be used on an organizational level, such as illegal interrogation tactics and organized crime, the tactics utilized on a personal, often one-on-one, level are some of the most interesting and malicious examples of dark psychology in practice today. The reason the Dark Triad is so closely associated with dark psychology is that these strategies are very often integrated and applied in their lives, almost like a natural talent. Their skills arise out of necessity and drive to acquire what they want from other people, but they have to devise manipulative tactics because they do not have the capacity or willingness to acquire them in acceptable ways. While the different personalities differ in key ways, one of the commonalities is that they are all willing to hurt other people in order to get what they want with little or no empathy involved. Because of the very nature of their willingness and coldness when it comes to other people, dark psychology tactics are a natural progression, as they often teach themselves as they identify their proclivities and natural talents.

But, you don't have to be a narcissist to be tempted to utilize dark psychology methods on others, even loved ones. And, sometimes, when personal motivations and desires are strong, we can all be susceptible to taking action and saying things that we regret later on. We have lied in order to make ourselves appear more attractive or more skilled, even if they were just "white" lies. This is a facet of dark psychology—you are leading someone to believe something that is not altogether true about you in order to achieve your desired result or impression. As I've said, the spectrum of use and application of dark psychology is a wide range and encompasses behaviors from the most benign white lie to the most sadistic mind games. It's important to realize this because people can fall back on dark psychology even without a history of malicious intent. When people become desperate or consumed by a desired outcome or goal, and none of the standard accepted ways of getting there are working, people can get a little devious in their methods. For example, in one of our chapters, we discuss seduction and the dark psychology that may be involved in a man trying to get a woman to come home with him or a similar scenario. When a man realizes that he lacks in one important area when it comes to social skills or relatability to women, he might employ dark psychology tactics simply because he sees no other feasible way to get what he wants. Some of these guys try their hand at lying to make themselves look good or flattery or some other tactic and fail miserably. Others learn to observe and learn about their targets before actually making their first moves. We will discuss in detail how the preparation phase of observation plays a key role in the successful outcome of dark psychology tactics as we move through this book.

Finally, I want to briefly discuss one of the less often acknowledged realities of dark psychology. That is the fact that everyone harbors an innate susceptibility and proclivity for both utilizing and falling prey to these tactics, whether you feel invulnerable and hyper-aware or not. Some very intelligent people have fallen prey to cult recruiters and are lucky enough to be able to share their experiences after the dark practices of the cult are revealed. People have an incredible capacity to practice denial when something they value or the realities they are comfortable with are threatened. It's the phenomenon where people refuse to believe something they don't want to believe, even if the overwhelming evidence is staring them in the face.

You have probably heard of some of the most famous psychology experiments from the 70s in which the darker sides of human nature were revealed. One of them involved taking volunteers and putting them in a situation where they were expected to inflict pain on another human being for the sake of science. The results were quite astounding and surprising. The experiment is referred to as the Milgram Experiment and originated from a man named Dr. Stanley Milgram, a psychologist at Yale University in 1961.

The experiment was controversial, not just because of the results but because of how the experiment was conducted. Volunteers were brought in and introduced to someone they thought was another volunteer but actually part of the experimenters' team. This person was required to employ a bit of acting skill. It was explained that this person would be hooked up to a machine on the other side of a wall—literally strapped and unable to move—while the volunteer would be operating the machine, which would inflict progressive intensities of brief electric shocks. The volunteer was asked to read off a series of questions to the man strapped to the chair. Each time the man answered incorrectly, the volunteer was instructed to press the button which would engage the electric shock. The voltage would increase as the man strapped to the machine answered more and more questions incorrectly. The experiment aimed to see how far people would go when they were pressured to follow instructions by an authority figure. The results might surprise you. No less than two-thirds of the experiment's participants progressed all the way to the infliction of a lethal level of electronic shock at 450 volts. And all of the participants were willing to progress up to 300.

The experiment was conducted shortly after the trial of a Nazi named Adolf Eichmann, and Milgram wanted to look more closely at this question regarding the Nazi's defense that he was "just following orders." How was it possible that seemingly benevolent and intelligent human beings could be convinced to engage in unethical practices toward others? The answers and theories arising from this question go beyond the scope of this book, but my point is that factors of which many of us are unaware can play a role in whether or not we fall victim to manipulative or coercive behaviors. When we deem an authority figure to know what they are doing and choose to place our trust in him, it becomes easier to get past certain levels of doubt and even pangs of warning coming from our conscience because we have formed a paradigm in our minds that associates only benevolent and trustworthy characteristics and intentions with this figure. There is also the element of peer pressure and the universal desire to not stick out in the crowd or be the one who is "different." This is an elementary facet of evolutionary instinct designed to support the social nature essential to human survival. When the Nazis donned those identical uniforms and associated themselves with an overarching philosophy that supported the success of their country, coupled with a charismatic speaker and leader in whom they learned to place their trust, those individuals soon found themselves in an environment where it became rather easy to overlook the unethical nature of their actions simply because of the sense of a greater purpose. Also, as part of a group, any blame and guilt they may have faced could be easily associated and placed on the group rather than the individual.

All of this is to say that none of us are exempted from the seduction of dark psychology. We all have desires and needs and aspirations, and sometimes, it is tempting to take the short cut when it comes to utilizing other people to our ends. The focus of this book is to open the door to awareness and understanding where these dark psychology strategies are concerned and open your eyes to the fact that the dark psychology practitioner does not always look the part. Even those whom you've trusted and loved for years can turn on you in the worst circumstances and use your love against you. This is the scary and tragic reality of dark psychology and one which you will master as you read on.

Chapter 2: How Prevalent Is Dark Psychology?

Now that we've discussed a bit about the different types of dark psychology which exist in society, we will now demonstrate how prevalent these practices really are in modern-day society. Because our idea of the dark psychology practitioner cannot be limited to obviously deviant or those with clear criminal intent, the

array of environments in which potential victims live out their day-to-day lives expands to include even those locations which might not be the first considered. We can imagine the dark alleyway or even a crowded bar as great hunting grounds for the predator employing dark psychology tactics, but oftentimes, our first encounters with dark psychology occur a little closer to home—inside the home, to be exact.

What we experience in our childhood often has a profound effect on how we turn out as human beings—what our values and morals are, how that reflects whatever religious or spiritual practices we were brought up around, how we treat and respect others, and whether or not we are taught to be afraid of or dislike those who are different from us—the list goes on and on. Though, we don't always turn out exactly as our parents had intended. Sometimes, this is a disappointment; other times, people break out of the antiquated, immoral practices or ways of thinking of their parents to become better, more informed people. These experiences can be rather benign and might include things like realizing as a teenager that you do not share the religious values your parents have taught you or the political views. Perhaps your parents wanted you to go to school and follow in their footsteps in terms of a career, but you soon discovered you didn't enjoy their occupation.

Sometimes, however, people experience hurtful behavior, verbal abuse, or both, which, over time, distorts their perception of how people should interact with one another. If, for example, a young boy was taught throughout his childhood that respect should be earned and trust shouldn't be given to just anybody, he may grow up to be very difficult to befriend and may have trouble trusting even those he cares about and has positive experiences with. Though it is not always the case, often, in unfortunate circumstances, young minds pick up on poor role model behavior, which may follow them around for the rest of their lives or until someone points it out and teaches them to behave differently at least. People may either be receptive to this re-teaching, or they may dismiss it out of hand. This is a character trait that might be attributed to equal parts genetics and upbringing. Let's look at a few examples.

If you enjoy documentaries or true crime, you've probably come across an interview or two where a professional who studies criminal behavior talks about things that happened in childhood that affected how he turned out as an adult. Childhood trauma, such as physical and sexual abuse, parents experiencing a messy divorce or fighting in front of the kids, alcohol or other substance abuse in the home, and many other examples can lead the child to emulate such behavior without a demonstration of other options. If there is nothing done about the influence of these poor role models in the home while a child is growing up, it can be very easy for the child to fall into the same behavior, especially since such experiences are often accompanied by the development of chronic mood disorders like depression, anxiety, difficulty dealing with anger, and personality disorders, the extreme of which have been cited previously, including sociopathic and narcissistic types.

Let us say a young boy named Johnny was sexually abused at the age of 10, and this abuse persisted in the next few years. Childhood and adolescent years are an integral time, not just for physical development, but also for emotional and mental development as well. People who have experienced sexual abuse often grow into adults with a distorted perception of the world and emotional reactions that are tied up with sexual stimulation. Johnny does not develop normally and finds no interest in girls, as all of his sexual stimulation, let's say, is stemming from an abusive male relative. He is too afraid to tell anyone, even his own family, as the perpetrator himself is a trusted member of that family. And this is a tragic reality when it comes to child abuse; children are easier to manipulate and often do not come forward because the perpetrator has played one of a variety of mind games on the child. One of these tactics is to inflict guilt and shame so that the child is too ashamed to come forward and blames himself for the abuse instead. Other children may be controlled by fear, being told that should they tell anyone else about what's going on, this abuser will hurt them more or hurt someone he loves, etc. There are plenty of harmful ways to control children, and this abuse is something that the child will likely carry with him or her for the rest of their lives, even if the abuse is brought to a stop and the perpetrator is brought to justice.

Going back to Johnny, as he develops sexually, his perception and experience with sex alters his patterns of thought and behavior in a way that reflects that experience. He may develop an association between violence and sex and also end up focusing his sexual attention on other young boys. This pattern persists even as he grows older because he has been essentially sexually stilted by this pattern of sexual and emotional abuse he suffered as a boy himself. All of these factors affect one and the other, which results in all sorts of adult deviant behavior and emotional reactions to sexual stimuli, many of which are completely inappropriate.

And, because the individual recognizes that his behavior is deviant, he must devise ways of getting what he wants through not-so-straightforward means, which leads to tactics of dark psychology. Johnny has learned from his own abuser how to condition and control others for sexual gratification, so he is likely more successful than he anticipated when he first puts these lessons into practice himself.

While the development of a personality that favors dark psychology is often cultivated in childhood, this is not always the case. Sometimes, it is learned later in life, when an individual feels he has exhausted all other means, those dark psychology tactics are the only way to achieve a goal. This goal might be money, power, control, fame, esteem, etc. We all tend to have desires along these lines, but most of us develop a corresponding framework of morality and values which would stop us, for example, from setting rumors all around the workplace in an effort to demean another coworker with whom we are in direct competition for a promotion, which brings me to the next area of society where dark psychology often runs rampant—the workplace.

Workplace politics are familiar to a lot of us through sitcoms, movies, social media, and real life. Most of us chuckle in commiseration when a friend tells us about a coworker who is annoying and quirky and who gets on her nerves, etc. We understand that it is very unlikely that we will go through our whole lives without ever having to deal with a difficult coworker or boss. But we make decisions and prioritize the things we care about in order to get past those things or people who are not so enjoyable to be around. And, if a situation at work is just too much to handle, we often make the decision to report behaviors to a boss, or we simply find a new job out of necessity. These actions take place following overt behavior, which is harmful to the company or other coworkers. But how about those things which we don't readily recognize are happening? This is where the clever practitioner of dark psychology tactics takes center stage.

While many strategies utilize the manipulation of people's negative emotions, such as fear and anxiety or shame in our last example with child abuse, sometimes, the strategies alternatively manipulate people's positive emotions in order to build up the practitioner on false pretenses. Skills, such as charisma and public speaking, often go hand-in-hand with these topics because it herds people together in a way that makes it easier to make the desired impression upon multiple people at once. A prime example is in a meeting at work or perhaps in a boardroom, where people might be more inclined to be followers of the outspoken, charismatic participant. These tactics might be used by a member of a team trying to take control or by the leader of the group, or, say, the CEO in a meeting with his underlings. The goal is to win the favor and trust, and respect of those who will prop him up where he wants to be. He can do this through a clever combination of flattery, peer pressure, personality mirroring, and many other strategies which, if done well, will not even be detectable by the people being affected.

These strategies involve paying close attention to the target or targets and basically telling them what they want to hear. It is basic yet complex. Especially when dealing with multiple people and multiple personalities, it becomes important to make each individual feel both unique and important but also to make them feel the pressure to adhere to the group, the rest of which is also in the process of being won over. People don't like to stick out or be different, especially in a work environment where, often, success and prominence depend on things like popularity and how well the person gets along with both coworkers and higher-ups.

As we've discussed, sometimes, dark psychology tactics arise out of necessity when an individual has a goal in conjunction with a limited or very low personal standard regarding ethics, principles, morals, etc. When something you want is more important than how you treat others, dark psychology can be the most effective and efficient way to get things done and achieve personal goals. Let us move into the bigger arena of politics to take a look at how this might—and does—manifest.

Anyone in the business will tell you that the world of politics can be one of the most aggressive, two-faced, and personally challenging work environments on the planet. This is because not every politician has only the good of his people in mind as his goal. We know through research and social experimentation that power and wealth have a strong correlation with corruption. Having these things plays with our psychology in a way that reinforces the idea that power and money and fame mean you are just "better" than anyone else, more capable, more intelligent, etc. This means that what you want and how you want to get there supersedes all other considerations because you believe you know best. Of course, I'm not saying every politician out there is crooked, but politics is definitely a rich ground for pulling out and examining dark psychology tactics in action.

Take the speech, for example. We talked about individuals in the boardroom who may consciously or unconsciously be able to control others' thoughts and opinions through charisma, public speaking skills, and tactics related to flattery and winning over others for personal gain. In political speech, this can happen on a massive scale, as a politician speaks to hundred, thousands, or tens of thousands of people at once. How does he accomplish what he wants to accomplish on this scale?

Obviously, it would be quite challenging to be able to speak a single speech and convince every single listener of the truth and validity of everything you've said, but he can be quite effective if he utilizes some key strategies. One strategy is a careful framing of information that paints your political agenda as much more correct, intelligent, and ethical than that of your opponents. In this strategy of persuasion, the speaker is appealing to the audience's sense of logic and reason. A statement is made; it sounds smart and follows logically. Therefore, the people in the audience begin nodding their heads in agreement. This must be done carefully, and it can't be a bald-faced lie that everyone in the audience knows is untrue. But there is an artful finesse to picking and choosing details involved in the facts and events to frame the event how you want it and how it will put you in a place that has an advantage over the opponent. The audience's emotions aren't really evoked in this strategy, but those who are looking for a candidate whom they feel is smart and capable may be affective greatly through this tactic.

But the politician rarely utilizes one strategy alone in this context. After all, he is trying to reach and persuade as many people as possible within his allotted 60 or 90-minute time slot. And, one of the quickest paths to persuading a complete stranger is through their emotions.

Have you ever seen a speaker open up his speech by telling a story about how he was brought up and how this motivated him to take action and improve the world in a specific way because of his childhood or adolescent experiences? This is a tactic that utilizes the audience's emotions and sensibilities in order to gain their attention and sympathy. The audience is placed in that situation through a brief storytelling episode, then brought emotionally to the conclusion that this individual is an honest man of integrity who is trying to correct something that is wrong in the world, with which he has direct experience. If the story is told in a moving and authentic way, this tactic can be the quickest way to potential voters' hearts.

Our next arena, into which we will go in more detail a little later in this book, is the arena of dating and seduction. Dark psychology strategies run rampant in this area of human society and to a wide array of varying degrees, some of which are quite innocent, while others can be deadly. Let us set the scene.

You are a young woman sitting at a bar alone. You didn't plan on being alone, but your friend is late getting out of work, and you said you would wait for her if she wanted you to. That was about 15 minutes ago.

You're drinking by yourself and absently staring at the TV set above the bar when a man approaches you and asks if he can sit down. He is smiling, well-dressed, and doesn't sound pushy, so you so "okay."

Your conversation is very casual and friendly. He isn't staring creepily at you and isn't using any cheesy pickup lines, so you decide he's nothing to worry about and enjoy your conversation with him. You start volunteering details that he didn't ask for, but you feel comfortable enough to let him know why you're here and that you're waiting for a friend. He starts to share details about his life with you as well. You are impressed that he is willing to show a little vulnerability as he describes how he had a hard day at work and is considering leaving his job for something better. He's dressed pretty nice, you think, so he can't be hurting too bad financially. He compliments how you look and tells you that you seem smart, and he is enjoying his conversation with you. At this point, you start to notice the beginnings of an attraction, and you decide it can't hurt to see where it might go. Your conversation turns a bit flirtatious, and you've had another drink at this time. You are feeling more and more loose and comfortable with this man. You've given him details about your life, but he's also given details about his, so you don't feel like you're being taken advantage of in any way. The thought crosses your mind that you might actually rather spend some more time with this man than hang out with your friend, and you ask if he wants to go somewhere quiet to talk. One thing leads to another from there.

So, what are the nuances to what just happened with this interaction that led to a fun night together with an attractive stranger? There might have been a lot more going on than meets the eye. Granted, there are certainly men out there who are naturally gifted in conversation with women, but a lot of men need to coordinate and plan carefully in order to get where they want to be, especially if they aren't the most attractive man in the room. Luckily for them, women can often be won over with personality and charm rather than looks, as they aren't so superficially inclined as a lot of men. This is where the dark psychology strategies come in.

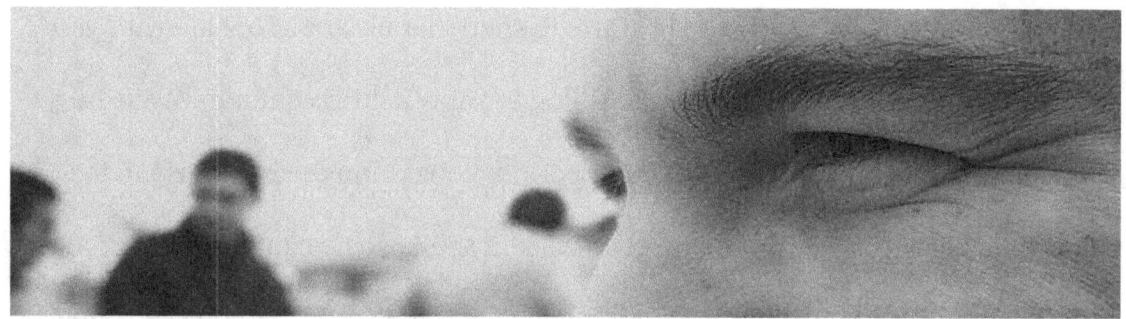

This man approached you in a casual, nonthreatening way. What you didn't realize is that this man has spent a good amount of time just watching you. He did this before approaching you to make educated guesses as to how you were feeling, what your personality might be like as you engaged with other people and the bartender, and whether or not you looked open to engaging in a conversation with a man. He decides that you looked slightly uncomfortable by yourself and guesses that you were probably waiting for someone who was running late to meet you. You probably weren't there specifically to find a date. By approaching casually and at an angle instead of straight toward you, he sent the message that he was just looking for a conversation to pass the time without any kind of agenda. He smiles and gestures in a friendly manner. Releasing personal information made you feel comfortable with letting your guard down a little, as he wasn't really coming on to you. As the conversation progressed, he was careful to share details about his life but also to listen to everything you had to say and engage with you to make you feel important and worth listening to. He listened and remained engaged, sending the message that he was really interested in everything you were talking about. By the end of the night, you decided you were in control of this situation and made the first move, which was exactly as he'd intended in the first place.

These examples we've discussed are just a few of the major areas where dark psychology is always at play in the modern world. Dating and seduction techniques extend to online platforms, as the use of social media makes it possible to groom from a distance and deceive on a whole new level. Young adults and teenagers are especially at risk of this type of predation because of their relative naïve natures and willingness to share information with detecting that someone might be trying to manipulate them.

As we move along, we'll encounter more specific situations and put dark psychology into context as it appears all around us today.

Chapter 3: How Do I Recognize When Dark Psychology Is Being Used?

Learning to recognize when strategies of dark psychology are at work can be a life-saving skill. Often, the situation is not so dire, but decades of research into dark psychology tactics and deviant personality types tell us that many of the most sinister criminals in American history have fallen under the umbrella  categorization of types that utilize dark psychology in order to lure victims to their fates. For example, serial killers are often cited as some of the most clever users of dark psychology tactics for the simple reason that, over time, they developed those skills for the sole purpose of scratching that itch they had to kill or abuse victims. Ted Bundy, perhaps one of the most well-known serial killers of all time, got very creative when it came to luring his victims, and a lot of his strategy relied on the "prep" work that took place even before he spoke to the victim.

The first stage of an intelligent practitioner's strategy for using dark psychology is one that remains invisible to the victims, or anyone else, for that matter. This is the observation stage. This is the time the practitioner sets aside to pay very close attention to potential victims in the area, whether he's already chosen his target or is watching the one he wants to zero in on. The target is observed, and the practitioner downloads everything he possibly can about the individual—her movements, the way she speaks to others, her apparent personality type, who she speaks to on a regular basis, where she works, her routines, and others. All of this information is useful for the practitioner trying to discover the most effective way to approach and put into practice whatever strategy he needs to get what he wants. The motivations for using dark psychology on other people are varied and different for each individual who decides to study another human being. This is part of what makes this reality so potentially dangerous. When you don't know the motivations, it is hard to predict behavior.

However, there are several things you can do to better prepare yourself for a dark psychology encounter, and you're already well on your way to fulfilling requirement one, which is educating yourself.

Dark psychology, in large part, depends on the victims not knowing what's going on, hence, "dark" psychology, as we explained in the introductory chapters. People's personalities and vulnerabilities vary from person to person, but, at the same time, there are certain universalities in terms of human behavior that the intelligent dark psychology practitioner exploits to the best of his ability. The whole process is a game, and if you remain one step ahead of your potential adversary, then you can avoid the harm and deceit that will follow an initial approach. Educate yourself and remain skeptical of strangers, especially if you get a bad feeling about the person approaching you.

The next basic practice, next to educating yourself on the basics and strategies of dark psychology, is to simply be aware that not everyone is who they present themselves to be. It is unfortunate that in this modern reality, we cannot really afford to trust our fellow men and women, but there are many people out there just looking and waiting for the opportunity to strike at an unsuspecting victim.

This is not to say that you should never develop new relationships and trust new people, but you should keep your guard up until you've received enough experience and evidence to make you feel comfortable and confident about offering another person your trust.

And it's not like untrustworthy people have never existed in the past. They have, of course, but the landscape of tools at the dark practitioner's disposal had expanded on a massive scale compared to just a few decades ago when there were no Facebook or social media to get an advantage on a target without anyone knowing. Social media, as has been revealed in recent years, can be used as a benevolent social connectivity tool but also for darker intentions that utilize false news stories and emotional manipulation. The 2016 election is a perfect example of what has recently been brought to light as this kind of dark, manipulative techniques in practice. Being aware and vigilant when it comes to allowing strangers to win over your trust and friendship is not different in the digital realm. If anything, you should be even more careful with people online than those you meet on the streets of a busy city.

The internet has provided a means for people all over the world to associate with one another in thousands of different contexts. People use the internet for work, social planning, meeting strangers with similar interests, and dating and meeting potential life partners. All of these require, to some degree, that you relinquish personal information, whether it's a simple email contact or someone whom you want to meet for the first time in person and find a nearby meeting place that is convenient for both of you. Those super popular personality quizzes all over social media provide a huge amount of data and information on people who willingly give this information out. This data doesn't just disappear once you're done with a quiz or whatever form you are filling out.

Data is the most lucrative business and commodity in the world—by a whole lot. And most people are completely unaware of what's going on when they login to their email accounts or go shopping online after clicking an ad on Facebook. Some people simply don't care. They enjoy the fact that they can be catered to and inundated with ads that are targeted to their specific interests. The fact is, there are incredibly detailed profiles of every single human being who is active online, and this information and data are bought and sold all over the place in order to learn how people tick — and then exploit it. Let's go back to the 2016 American presidential election as an example.

The last couple of elections has seen a whole new era emerge in which voters are no longer engaged through in-person campaigning and simple TV ads with a focus on reaching as wide of an audience as possible. With today's connected world and the oceans of data floating around on millions of people all over the country, it has become possible to pinpoint exactly where those voters are. These voters can be persuaded to one political side or the other, "persuadable," and to target them directly through online ads designed to incite fear, anger, empathy, or whatever else seems useful in the endeavor. There is dark psychology going on here, even if there is no face-to-face interaction, and it is very effective.

People who were on the fence in 2016 saw a barrage of misleading or extremely one-sided ads pop up on their Facebook feeds, which sent messages designed to make them see the world the way the advertisers wanted them to. Trump's opponent was painted as an extreme criminalistic individual with ads supporting the tag line "lock her up" and many others. Fake news stories were disseminated in order to convince people of a certain reality and to incite fear and anxiety about whatever the designers wanted them to. People like to think that they are above such psychological ploys and that they are making their own informed decisions, but a lot of us have no idea just how impressionable we all really are, and that is a dangerous reality. Many activists today are trying too hard to eradicate this kind of conduct, especially centering around political elections, and support the idea that personal data should be every person's right and should be protected just like any physical property. This would be one of the greatest challenges a person or organization could ever undertake simply because of the massive presence and ethereal nature of personal data.

So, what can you personally do to protect yourself from certain infringements on your personal data? The answer, to some degree, is nothing. However, you can be proactive in terms of protecting your accounts and taking advantage of all the security measures which are available for people to use online. Banks and credit card companies don't want to put your assets at risk, though people have their credit card numbers stolen all the time. Being vigilant with how you use your cards and personal information online is essential to protect yourself from online fraud. Only use your information on trusted and protected sites. Don't visit sites you don't trust and don't engage in personal conversations with strangers until you have developed a relationship and met them in real life. A person can tell you anything you want to hear from the safety of hiding behind an anonymous screen. Online dating sites have brought people together, and there are lots of wonderful relationships in existence today, which started online, but there are also countless tragedies that have started online, through dating or social media sites. Children and teenagers are especially at risk, as they are often much easier prey than adults who are aware and have experienced the personal dangers involved with interacting with people online. Do not meet someone for the first time in your home or agree to go to their home. Always meet in public until you've developed trust and feel confident you know the person well. Trust your instincts, above all. Don't dismiss a random "bad feeling" if you start to feel this way. Sometimes our subconsciousness knows even more than we think we do about situations and people around us. This is an essential tool when it comes to being approached by a potential dark psychology practitioner as well. The idea of "innocent until proven guilty" does not apply in personal interactions, and you should be on your guard at all times when out in public or when meeting new people.

There is a balance between being able to protect yourself and being open to helping others and forming relationships that develop quickly. While you want to remain aware of all possibilities in public situations and when interacting with people you don't know, you also don't want to cultivate a lifestyle where you are living in fear and seem completely unable to develop trust for people outside of your current circle of family and friends. We, as human beings, are social creatures, and we thrive on developing relationships and being to relate our experiences to those of other people in conversation or other scenarios. Don't be afraid to engage in a conversation with that intriguing man at the bar during a party, but simply be careful about the information you are freely giving out. The group of people actively waiting for an opportunity to manipulate others is much smaller than the group with people who are simply looking to make connections and relate to someone. Don't shut everyone out who crosses your path if you feel like you might be interested in getting to know someone.

A good rule to adhere to in a public situation is never to get drunk with a stranger or group of strangers. This might seem obvious as you sit here and read the statement, but a master manipulator will use whatever he can to make a person feel comfortable enough to drink to the point where they are no longer making good decisions for themselves. If you are at a party or in an atmosphere where there is drinking and partying, always stick close by a friend whom you really know and trust. Don't ever go to a party by yourself where you are obviously alone and vulnerable. Again, it is unlikely, in most situations, that someone is just waiting for someone like that to walk in so he can manipulate you into something you don't want to do, but the chance that there is a manipulator around should be enough to encourage utilizing every safety precaution. When you are accompanied by someone you trust, you are not only protecting yourself, but you are also placing yourself in a position where you can keep an eye on your friend and be her protector as well.

As a side note, I use male pronouns a lot when talking about dark psychology, but women are just as capable and ruthless when it comes to utilizing dark psychology for personal gain. Statistically, there are many more males in the population of violent criminals who fall into the categories of narcissist or sociopath. But it is not unheard of for a female to be the aggressor in an insidious dark psychology situation, perhaps with a significant other or family member. The fact that we hear more about male perpetrators and manipulators than women does not mean that those females do not exist in the population. There is simply a different set of tools at the woman's disposal, and they are used a little bit differently.

In addition to learning all you can about dark psychology strategy, it is also very helpful to understand, as much as possible, about human nature and how people can become vulnerable in social situations. We've touched on several at work according to different purposes.

In the common scenario of a man trying to pick up a woman in a public setting, flattery and charm are often used in order to get the woman to lower her guard and feel good about the budding relationship. Knowing ahead of time that things  like flattery have a very real effect on emotions and decision-making will help give you a bit of an advantage if this situation unfolds for you. The same is true in the reverse situation. Women can use flattery and charm and make a complete stranger feel like a superhero in a very short amount of time. This is because we are all susceptible to the positive feelings that arise when someone is complimenting us. We simply can't help it, and you shouldn't feel like a weak-minded person when this happens. The key is to recognize what's going on and not fall into a trap where you are releasing additional information to this person simply because he or she makes you feel good. It could be sincere, as we have mentioned, but it might be an act.

If you are with a friend and someone is approaching him or her, and you get a bad feeling about the interaction, don't be afraid to interrupt on your friend's behalf. Some people may be hesitant in this scenario and feel that it isn't his or her place to get in between what might look like a really pleasant interaction. But, if this person is really your friend, take it upon yourself to protect him or her from potential predatory threats, especially if there is alcohol involved. You can do this by staying nearby and not actually interrupting in an explicit sense. If you can, keep an eye on the interaction and observe how your friend is behaving and interacting. Is she drinking more than she should? Does it look like this person is showing her compliments and flattery? These are such common tactics; it is worth looking into if you suspect that the person's intentions are not completely benign.

The last topic to discuss in terms of recognizing dark psychology in action is a much more difficult one to deal with and, often, is not recognized until things have escalated to a point where someone is really getting hurt, emotionally or physically. I'm talking about dark psychology in practice that involves a close friend, family member, or colleague. It is a much simpler issue to discuss how you can protect yourself from complete strangers, but what can you do when it is your own family member or partner? This can be an incredibly painful and complex problem to solve, but the most common impairment in this situation on the part of the victim is the factor of denial.

We simply don't want to believe that someone we have loved and trusted for a long time is capable of harmful and manipulative techniques. The abusive husband, the son who is a drug addict, the domineering mother or father — all of these situations can be crippling for life for the victim if the behavior is never recognized or addressed.

Perhaps the first thing to wrap your mind around in this situation is that no one is perfect, no one is an angel, and we all have hang-ups. If someone you love and trust tries to gaslight you and put you in a state of confusion, you have to recognize that this is really happening and that, in many cases, you simply can't "fix" other people when they make the decision to use these dark psychology strategies. Narcissists don't magically rid themselves of narcissism when someone speaks reason to them. Neither does the sociopath, in most cases. Someone who is manipulative has chosen this lifestyle because he or she has been able to get what he or she wants in the past using these tools. It's as simple as that. It may be incredibly painful to realize, but it is imperative that an individual removes herself from the situation as soon as possible when she recognizes that things don't seem quite right and there are inconsistencies in her partner's or friend's behaviors. Red flags have to be paid attention to—it could save your life or the life of someone you know and love.

In the following chapters, we will get into deeper detail about specific manipulative techniques and several different examples of motivations that can lead someone to engage in these techniques as the most efficient way to achieve a goal or get what a person wants from others.

Chapter 4: Manipulation Techniques

Manipulation itself comes in many forms, along with varying intentions and motivations. Some of them are used with malicious intent, while other people simply use the principles of persuasion in order to make a sale or convince someone of their point of view. Dark psychology is often brought into discussion when we are talking about the absolute worst example of manipulation tactics, though technically, magicians using sleight of hand to impress a group of children is a dark psychology technique.

I make this point as we move on to discuss specific techniques so that you have a broader idea of what we are discussing when we say dark psychology and manipulation. It is likely that you did not pick up this book to learn about magicians' technique, so you will notice that most of the dark psychology techniques we discuss in this book are used most often for decidedly malicious or selfish reasons on the part of the dark psychology practitioner. Let us begin with persuasion.

Persuasion

Aristotle outlined three modes of persuasion under the terms logos, pathos, and ethos. Each of these persuasion modes is a good illustration of the different ways people try to "get in" with other people with the specific intention of getting them to believe the same way you do about a certain belief system or to get something from them willingly that they had not been inclined to give before the conversation began. As we discussed earlier, there are many different paths available to take in order to fulfill this goal. You can appeal to a person's sense of logic, you can appeal strictly to emotions, or you can appeal to others by giving the impression that you are someone others should follow based on things like strong character, charisma, morals, and ethics, etc. Logos is the term related to appealing to logic, ethos is related to appealing to emotions, and pathos is the strategy of presenting yourself as a strong and worthy leader for others to follow. Each of these is effective in different ways, and oftentimes they are used in conjunction in order to reach lots of different people and personalities at the same time. We can see all of these strategies in action by looking at the example of a political speech.

In a speech where there are many gathered to listen, it is quite impossible to pinpoint one singular strategy that is likely to touch everyone listening in the exact same way. For this reason, most speechwriters are going to aim to cover a lot of ground in terms of persuasive techniques so that they gain as much attention and affinity toward the candidate as possible.

When it comes to stirring people's emotions, many speakers will move toward storytelling as a way to demonstrate where the person's heart is and where their motivations are coming from for running for office and the things they hope to accomplish while in office. If the speaker can make an emotional connection, and listeners believe that he is sincere, then they will gradually start to view the speaker as pure of the heart where that particular issue is concerned. They experienced something that made them take action to improve the situation for anyone else who might have to go through what he went through, etc. Motivation like this comes off as pure and honest, and kind-hearted, and this can often be enough to move a voter who is on the fence towards this particular candidate's side in an election.

Logos is an approach thats focuses on appealing to the collective audience's logic and reason. The speaker will present his views in a way that makes sense or what appears to make sense. Arguments and framing facts is an art in itself, which often entails picking out details and facts here and there, which serve to prop up the speaker's views and opinions and omits anything that might plant a seed of doubt in the listeners' minds. This is something that politicians and talking heads often call "spin." Politicians and their writers often spin the facts to make their own positions look like the logical, correct side to be on. Logical arguments must follow a line of reasoning that makes sense to the listener. Otherwise, there is no impact. The speaker doesn't want to make anyone listening to him feel too dumb to understand, but he also wants to make himself look like he really knows what he's talking about. The use of facts and figures, statistics, and citing what most people recognize as a reputable source of information are all things that will help prop the logical argument.

Finally, in a pathos line of argument, the focus is on how the speaker himself is being presented. What is the first impression you want to make on those people in the audience who are looking at you, watching your mannerisms, and hearing you speak? When the pathos mode is active, there is usually a great deal of attention given to how the speaker looks, down to the last detail. What clothes is the speaker wearing? What does this say about him or her? What details might suggest positive things to those watching? Believe it or not, there is a great deal of evidence in research to suggest that people are often swayed to voting for someone based on how much better they look physically than their competitors.

And this often becomes a factor even when it is not obvious or apparent to the person making the judgment. People are drawn to those who look healthy and fertile, and this often means the younger candidates with handsome features and better skin have an automatic leg up on the competition if they are deemed not as good-looking.

But aside from how the speaker looks, a lot of attention is given to how the speaker will interact with the audience, not just concerning the specific words coming out of his mouth but how he will move and use body language to convey an impression he wants from the listeners. A lot of this body language is recorded and has an influence on a subconscious level, which we will discuss in more detail in a later chapter. How often will the speaker use his hands, make eye contact, or use gestures to elucidate what he is saying?

The words in his speech themselves will be focused on forming a reflection of good character and whatever else the politician wishes to convey to his audience. The words must be chosen carefully to avoid sounding like boasting without enough foundation or evidence. The ideal impression would be that a listener finds the speaker charismatic, sincere, and honest about his goals for the future and for his political party. If the candidate is a veteran, this will likely be a highlight of the speech as an introduction according to the pathos mode of persuasion. The audience already has a great deal of information and data, which automatically connotes with the word "veteran," and so a lot of the work will be done for the speaker just by mentioning the specifics of when and where he served. Other categorizations work in a similar way, such as working for nonprofit and charity organizations connoting generosity and kind-hearted, selfless nature.

Pathos, logos, and ethos can all work on much smaller scales and in a one-on-one situation. The salesman who has a couple of minutes of interaction on the sales floor with potential customers will employ tactics that engage the person's emotions through need. He will often pitch the customer in the form of a well-reasoned argument for why the product will bring some benefit to the customer's life, and he will also portray himself as someone whom the customer can trust and respect based on a professional, congenial, and friendly demeanor and mannerisms.

Taking Over a Room/Becoming "Alpha"

This area of manipulation happens on a group scale that is not necessarily as large as a political speech. When we talk about the alpha of a group, we're talking about the unspoken (or spoken) dominant individual in a group, male, who is the leader, most popular, etc. The term is used to describe a person with many dominant personality traits. Here, we'll talk about the process of winning over a group of people who had been strangers and are now aware and interested in this individual. These tactics are often used in a situation when a practitioner wants to gain the attention of someone in the room. Perhaps there is someone important present who could help the individual move forward at work or in some other endeavor. Or perhaps there is a woman he wants to get the attention of, but she is always surrounded by people and tends to favor the popular, powerful type. For any of these reasons, the following plan of action is often cited as a strategy that can work like magic within as little as a few hours.

As with pretty much every successful practitioner of dark psychology tactics, this individual—let's call him John—has put in some prep work. He has gathered as much information as he possibly could through observation, perhaps a little online digging to check out social media profiles, etc. He gets familiar with the type and function of the gathering itself. Is it primarily social? What kind of people are the most important ones there? Who is hosting? Who are the influential figures that will be present? Before the event, John must have a singular, focused goal for his actions. Let's say he is trying to win over the CEO at his company because there is a potential position opening up that would come with a substantial pay raise, and John really wants to be considered. There is a lot of competition in the form of very talented and skilled employees as well as people who have been with the company for a very long time. John has worked at the company long enough to know that the people in power like motivation, drive, charisma, and the ability to talk smoothly and with confidence, especially when it comes to meetings with potential clients.

John's first action of preparation is to be sure to dress the part. He pays attention to cleanliness, his teeth are sparkling white, and his clothes are freshly cleaned and ironed. He might choose to invest in a brand that is similar to the type of clothing he's seen his higher-ups wear on the occasions he's interacted with them. Mirroring will come into play a little later, and subtle things like wearing similar clothing will play into this specific tactic nicely.

The next important consideration is to make sure he arrives promptly at the start of the event. He doesn't want to show up too early, which could be annoying and inconvenient, and he doesn't want to show up too late, which might signal disinterest and turn off those people who have already had better impressions from the other competition. Now it's time to mingle.

The goal for the next hour or so is for John to go around and introduce himself to as many people as he possibly can. He doesn't just go shake hands with them and move on.

Rather, he introduces himself to one, and then the rest of the circle then listens to what the conversation topic is at the moment of his arrival. He will stand with confidence, shoulders back, head up, and listen to what's going on. Careful not to interrupt or appear rude, he waits for an opportune time to interject with something very thoughtful, intelligent, or witty. If he doesn't really know much about what's being talked about, he might fall back on being entertaining through a well-timed joke, or he might give compliments to the speakers and express interest in the topic which he could learn more about or, even better, all of these things within the same conversation. In these few minutes, he has now managed to make himself known to this group, expressed an interested and entertaining personality, and ingratiated himself to the speakers by complimenting their intelligence. All of these things are moving him forward, even if he hasn't directly addressed his main target yet.

As human beings, we are very social animals, and we take a lot of cues about how to feel about other people by the way others react and interact with that individual. How often have you been in the middle of a crowd where one person starts talking loudly about someone nearby who smells bad or is dressed weird, and people all around within earshot start looking around and automatically making grimacing facial expressions as if they are the ones who have directly interacted with this weird, smelly individual. We are more susceptible to social influence than a lot of us like to think, and this overconfidence is something someone like John will be taking advantage of over time.

Once John feels he has met his goals with this first group, he moves on to the next. It is important for John's success that he does not from go group to group, repeating the exact same comments and behaviors as the group before. There may be a lot these people have in common, but they are all individuals, too, with unique personalities, insights, and behaviors. The next group may be talking about a completely different topic about which John has some knowledge. Again, without interrupting or completely hijacking the conversation, he waits for a good moment to slowly involve himself in the conversation. But he is careful not to spout facts and figures to impress people with his knowledge. One of the main things at the front of John's mind is that at the end of the day, people just want to be entertained. If he can be entertaining, he is going to be remembered. No one really remembers the boring guy who could recite a bunch of boring information like he's reading from a book. While it might be impressive, that probably isn't what most of the attendants are looking to spend their time doing. As John speaks, he is also careful to listen and ask people questions as he goes along. He knows that people really respond well to a few specific things when it comes to casual conversation—talking about themselves and hearing their own names. John will involve both tactics in his conversation rounds as he works his way around the room.

What starts to happen during this process is that John is making positive impressions all around the room with many different guests. As he moves, he might even be starting to get people to follow him around the room with interest in what he has to say further. He may stop at the refreshments table to interact with whoever is standing there, taking the opportunity to say something funny as he takes the measure of the different personalities. Again, he is careful not to just repeat his behavior and comments with everyone in the room. He may come up against someone who does not look like she is having fun and instead approaches with a little less of the pep he has carried with him thus far. He might express that he's noticed she doesn't look like she's having fun and ask if there is something bothering her and if she would like to talk about it. Another tactic would be to say something funny and see if he can get a positive reaction out of her. This would be a big win, as anyone who has ever been in a bad mood often appreciates someone who can chase away the clouds, even if it's just for a few minutes.

And finally, the moment arrives when he has the opportunity to meet and interact with his main target. If all has gone well up to this point, John may be brought over by someone who has taken a liking to John and offers to introduce them. This will likely resonate with John's target. Let's call him Mr. Carter. Mr. Carter sees the enthusiasm being exuded from John's acquaintance, and this sends a positive signal to Mr. Carter's subconscious that this John fellow might be alright, even if he isn't directly aware of it.

John is introduced, and now, he must up his game and become hyper-focused. Again, the skill of observation is going to be very important here. John must show interest in his target's words and actions, as well as offer an entertaining yet knowledgeable and charismatic interaction. One of the key strategies he may use here, and which is used widely in similar situations, is the tactic of mirroring.

Mirroring is all about assimilating subtle mannerisms, behavior patterns, and aspects of someone's personality into your own behavior and speech patterns as you are speaking with the target. The reason this works to help you ingratiate yourself quickly to a target is that human beings on a fundamental, evolutionary level respond more positively to things and people that appear and feel familiar. It is a signal of safety and of like-mindedness that will bypass any negative impressions, assuming it is done in a way that does not look like mocking. This would be a disaster, as no one likes to be mocked, and it would be a major insult, to destroy all the gain John has made at the party so far.

For this reason, effective mirroring is very subtle. John doesn't want to look like he's mocking Mr. Carter, but he wants to move into a position where he will recognize and appreciate certain important commonalities. Some of the safe ways to do this include sharing similar political views, opinions on business practice, past experiences, and personality traits. The personality traits, which will be the most forthcoming upon first interacting with Mr. Carter, will reflect how outgoing, personable, and open he is. If Mr. Carter is having a good time and uses lots of big gestures, like opening his hands and using his hands to gesture while he is talking, then John needs to get on his level and appear outgoing, motivated, and like he is having a good time. He will also make his points with enthusiasm, using lots of gestures to mirror Mr. Carter's passion for his own views.

On the other hand, if Mr. Carter is quite reserved and conservative in his conversation style, John will mirror this environment and keep his conversation and interactions reserved, though he might take a risk and tell a joke in order to be entertaining once he feels he's established some level of rapport with his target.

At the end of the interaction, John should have a pretty good idea of how he is doing based on Mr. Carter's progression throughout the conversation. Has he continued on and progressively become more open in his topics? Has he released information that he might not have if he didn't feel comfortable with John? These and many more are questions that will go through John's mind as the conversation comes to an end. He will also pay close attention to how Mr. Carter chooses to end the conversation. An open invitation or movement toward a second meeting is a great signal, and this will tell John that the interaction has been successful.

There are many other possibilities for dark psychology tactics that may have been present in just this one night's event, and we will continue to touch on others and progress through how these might play out in different scenarios. On a conversational level, there are less covert but no less effective tactics that people practice on a daily basis, even if they aren't overtly trying to win someone over for a specific goal that they are aware of.

Flattery is one of the most common things people use to get on people's good sides, whether they are trying to pick up a date or form new friendships and alliances. People enjoy flattery when it doesn't feel like the person is trying too hard and being insincere. Think of a time when you were in line at a store or other public place, and a complete stranger takes the time to stop and compliment you on something. Maybe you look nice in your outfit, or they like your hairstyle, etc. This feels good because someone had gone out of their way to address a stranger when there really wasn't anything to gain from the measure. It can turn your whole day around when someone compliments you like this. It feels just as good to receive compliments at work from coworkers or when you are out with your friends. When it is done right, flattery can instantly ingratiate someone who had simply been a complete stranger before and move them quickly into the realm of acquaintance. However, flattery can also go sideways when the target picks up on the fact that you were only flattering them as a precursor to asking for something. We see this played out in sitcoms all the time when a character approaches the boss and offers a silly compliment before asking for something that he is pretty sure the boss will say no to. If he can "butter him up" first, he knows there is some slight possibility he will

improve his chances of getting what he wants. This can really put a person off if this tactic is revealed and the behavior is too obvious, and he may completely shut down the conversation as he realizes he is being duped.

Online Grooming

The last area of dark psychology tactics we'll discuss in this chapter pertains to online behaviors and interactions. Relative to other dark psychology realms and tactics, this arena is new and still being researched and explored, especially in relation to how people interact and form relationships online.

Grooming refers to a practice where a person talks to a target, usually young and naïve, in the most successful instances, and develops a relationship with them online. Tragic accounts relay the succession of events in detail, as will the following.

A young girl named Amanda is very active online with social media accounts, and she constantly posts things on Facebook, Instagram, Twitter, and other sites, which give her followers a pretty good idea of how she spends her time from day to day and who she likes to interact with. She enjoys taking selfies and making herself look as cool and pretty as possible. She also uses filters and such which make her look more attractive, and she likes how sometimes she can make herself look older and more mature from the right angle.

An online predator will often look for signs like this as a way to pinpoint prospective victims, but it also has a lot to do with the wrong place at the wrong time. A predator attracted to an individual decides to move on his plan to groom her through flattery and constant attention. When this is shut down right away, often, the predator will simply move on. But if the grooming is successful, the predator will receive positive signals that his ploy is working when the attention he is offering is acknowledged almost all the time, and there are positive responses. The online groomer will continue these interactions and slowly introduce suggestions that move the relationship further. At first, just innocently 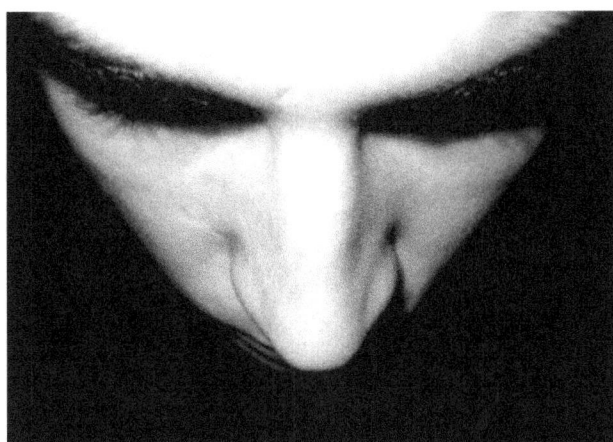 flirting and constantly bantering are the main interactions going on. But then, he will throw out a more sexually-oriented comment to see if the young teenager takes the bait. If she does, then he's got a green light to keep going, as this child seems to be fooled. If the child is put off by the comment by not responding to the predator, he might hold back and slow things down until he can reform that sense of trust and comfort that was presented before. Some predators spend a great deal of time online talking to young women under the pretense of being someone they are not. They follow those leads which seem promising and abandon those that don't seem to be going anywhere.

The ultimate goal in a lot of these grooming instances is to get the child to agree to meet in person somewhere that is private, like the predator's home. Agreeing to something like this suggests a very strong degree of trust and naivete about the possibility that someone is pursuing something he shouldn't. In her mind, she is meeting with a cute, playful young guy who is attractive. Perhaps this will be her first boyfriend, and she blinded by the excitement of it all. Some of these cases end in very tragic ways, and this reinforces the importance of getting the message through to young people that they can't trust everyone they meet online and that they should be very wary of this grooming tactic so that they recognize it if it happens to them. Many kids have interacted online with a predator who has moved on, and they never have any idea that this was what took place.

Chapter 5: What Is Mind Control?

When most people hear the phrase "mind control," they associate things they might have heard in the movies or on a TV show. It sounds like a science-fiction concept, and there are plenty of people who do not believe that it is possible to control another person's mind. And to some degree, they are correct. But the term mind control does not mean the same thing to everyone, and when psychologists use the term, they are not talking about turning another human being into a robot for personal use. The arts surrounding mind control are much more subtle and more powerful than most people are familiar with.

Mind control reached public consciousness through media like science fiction movies, but there are practices which can have a direct influence on a subject's psychological state. Even the manipulation techniques through social media ads is a form of mind control in which there is a subtle influence going on that the target is completely unaware of. The idea of mind control practices is not to turn a human being into an automaton but to influence decision-making on a level where the individual believes they are making the decision or reacting under their own volition. Let's look at a few different examples of mind control.

Hypnosis

Hypnosis is another term that comes with a lot of connotation straight from science fiction movies. When people are hypnotized in movies or TV shows, they are often completely catatonic and under complete control of the hypnotist. This is certainly untrue, but there is a great misunderstanding in the greater culture about the nature and intention of hypnosis.

Hypnosis is often used in the context of treatment for people who are suffering from memory impairment as a symptom of a bigger problem. It can also be used as a form of therapy in order to work through traumatic experiences and encourage the movement of emotional processing, like grief.

The hypnosis therapist is not someone with special power over people's brains. Their practice rather stems from full engagement and openness to empathy directed toward a patient for different means. The essential ingredient to a successful hypnosis therapy is an established trust and respect between therapist and patient. The patient goes into the process with an understanding that her part in the process is not just to sit back and let things happen. The patient has a responsibility to open up to the process and allow herself to become vulnerable and impressionable. She goes willingly and follows the therapist, where he leads. So, in this way, there is a partnership going on with in the process instead of this popular notion that the therapist can simply put people under a "spell." In fact, there are plenty of people who are simply less impressionable and open to the process of hypnosis, and therefore, would see no benefit from an attempt.

In a hypnotic session which aims to reach back and pull memories from a patient's mind, which has put up a barrier to protect it from painful experiences, the hypnosis therapist gently guides the patient, over time, close to the origin of those memories that are trying to be retrieved. The patient must let go and be willing to follow the instructions and suggestions, almost like someone leading her by the hand as she walks through memory lane. In this way, the patient may be able to stumble upon memories of repressed experiences that are working to hold her back or hurt her emotionally, seemingly without her control. Once these repressed memories can be addressed, the patient can work past the pain through therapy and refresh her mind to come to a place where she is fully functional and able to process and develop new memories and emotions.

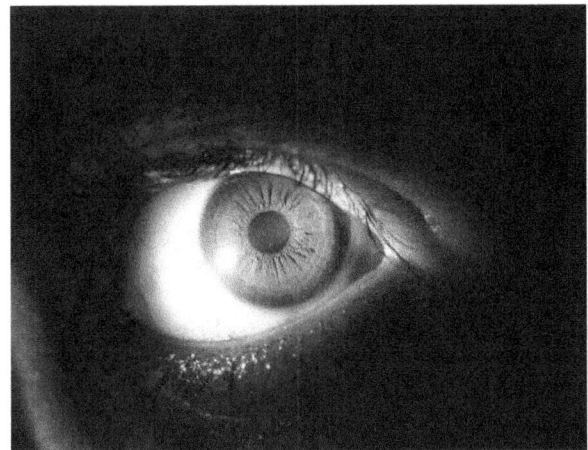

Hypnosis is also used to treat patients who suffer from PTSD through engaging with and working through repressed experiences or experiences which haunt the patient day and night. Each process is different, as well as individual outcomes. Hypnosis has become quite stigmatized, and many people look at the process with a skeptical view, but there are others who praise the process of hypnosis, claiming the process is responsible for great recoveries through consistent practice.

Gaslighting

Next, let's take a look at a much more insidious form of mind control—that of gaslighting. If you've never heard the term gaslighting, then count yourself fortunate for never having had to experience it. Or, perhaps you just didn't recognize or know there was a term for this particular manipulative technique.

Gaslighting refers to a process where the abuser convinces the victim over time that what he or she believed was real is questionable. Often, this happens through a long series of denials, in which the victim tries to get an abuser to acknowledge wrongdoing while the abuser consistently denies that any abuse is going on. At first, the victim may be enraged and become insistent, throwing the clear evidence or the facts she knows to be true in the abuser's face, but the abuser remains steadfast in his denials. Over time, this confrontational attitude deteriorates, and the victim is broken down. After a while, the once confident and confrontational victim starts to succumb to doubts and confusion as to what he or she is actually experiencing. The effects of this kind of abuse are long-lasting and often intense, especially if the abuse is happening during childhood or adolescent years.

When a parent or guardian engages in gaslighting, the child becomes incredibly confused and ashamed that he or she cannot grasp what is going on. This damage can extend to the child's personality as well as his or her emotional intelligence and development. This kind of abuse is not something that a person gets over quickly with a few sessions of therapy. It is also one of the most dangerous forms of long-term manipulation because of the mental damage that can be inflicted.

Gaslighting can also be just one ingredient in a potent cocktail of manipulation techniques, which work together with other tactics in order to enforce control and manipulate a partner in a romantic relationship. Once a bond of love and trust is formed, partners who suddenly switch gears and become abusive can be incredibly hurtful and wield power to inflict a large amount of pain and suffering on the partner or those who love the abuser. We hear in the news sometimes about an abusive husband or a domestic situation where the victim in the partnership simply refuses to let go or get out of the situation. Sometimes we may be tempted to judge these individuals as if to say, "why doesn't she just leave?" The truth is, there is often a whole lot more going on than meets the eye.

If the situation were simple, then perhaps we can imagine an abuser coming straight out one day out of the blue and beginning to abuse his wife. The wife sees the behavior, knows she is in danger, and then leaves immediately to stay with a friend or other family member. But domestic abuse situations are rarely so simple. There are mind games that are likely being played on the part of the abuser, and these games can work their way deep into a victim's mind so that the victim may believe preposterous things about the situation or remain in complete denial that there is anything serious happening. Let's look at an example scenario to see how this might play out to get a better understanding of these mind games.

Mandy is a newlywed and has just married her high school sweetheart, Danny. They are young and in love and reflect that kind of puppy love that makes it seem like the two of them just can't get enough of each other. They are both looking for jobs and for an apartment to move into. During high school, there was a structure that supported them, and their parents have been helping out to the best of their abilities. They don't have children yet, and they are planning to become financially stable before planning for a family.

Abuse and domestic turmoil often follow an event or series of events in which the  structure and support that the couple had been used to have been destroyed or changed in some way, and they could not seem to go back. This could happen in the form of a job opportunity falling through, an unexpected child getting in the way, parents who stop supporting the kids financially, or suffering from death in the family. All these are example situations that might upend all the couple's plans for the near future. When something drastic happens to change a person's way of life at a time when they don't have someone to lean on or some kind of support network, the consequences can be severe and long-lasting. In this case, we have a young couple who is in love but have yet to face any real-life challenges that marriage and life after school often entail. Abuse may begin to rear its head after the initial period known as the "honeymoon" phase, which is the time when everything feels perfect because you are consumed by love for the other person.

Their underlying personality traits have not shown up yet because both partners are still trying to put their best feet forward and present the best of what they are in order to be as attractive as possible.

But marriage isn't about only seeing the best parts of people. And sometimes, there are things about a spouse that are much darker or completely unexpected. It is during this time that the couple goes through a real-time of growing pains, in which they must decide what they really want out of a partner and whether or not they can accept the person's perceived flaws through the strength of their bond.

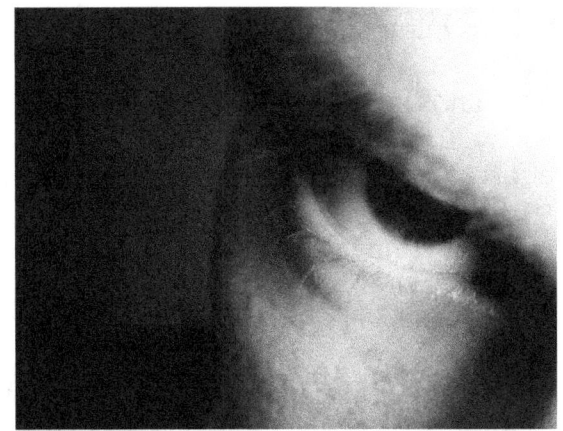

In Mandy and Danny's case, Danny starts off by just becoming distant as the months pass by as he is looking for stable work. They are no longer in school, and Mandy is looking at college opportunities in the area. Perhaps Danny is really struggling much more than Mandy, but he feels like he can't tell her about it because it makes him feel weak. Instead, he lets his anxiety and emotions fester until he is driven to take them out on someone.

Danny becomes verbally abusive, and Mandy fights back, contributing to some of the worst fights they've ever had in their short relationship. At this point, personality traits are coming to light that perhaps neither of them have seen before in themselves. As Mandy begins to push away, Danny sees that he is on his way to losing his wife if he can't convince her to stay. He may go into a panic mode and begin reaching toward manipulation as a response to this anxiety, or he may decide that control is the only way to calm himself down. The impetus for turning to manipulative and controlling techniques in a relationship can be one of a myriad of different things, but often, the action comes from fear of losing the partner, rooted in jealousy, or a fear of being alone.

In the beginning, Danny may even be successful in convincing himself that he is not manipulative, but anyone on the outside might see differently, having seen what is happening. Danny begins to beg forgiveness after he has hurt his young wife, and the two of them engage in long conversations after their fights in an effort to reconcile; and Danny assures Mandy that he won't behave that way again and everything will be alright. He showers her with love in these moments, and she believes his words because of a combination of wanting to believe him and the effort he's put into coming off as completely sincere. In the back of his mind, he may truly think that he is getting past these behaviors, but if the anxiety and underlying mood disorder are not addressed, then there is nothing to stop this pattern of emotional reaction in the face of acute stress.

The next time they fight, he abuses her verbally and calls her harsh names that he has never used before. The anger feels more intense and uncontrollable, but again, after a while, they end up talking and getting through the night, agreeing that they still love each other. The last time this happened, emotional manipulation through flattery and expressions of love worked to calm his wife down, so he engages in these practices again, even if he doesn't feel them to be completely true. He is prideful and doesn't want to acknowledge any possibility that his anger and frustrations may be getting out of control. In an effort to distract himself, he pulls away from his wife and sees that when he does this, she becomes desperate and willing to do anything to get him to come back and open up to her. He sees that he can use this to his advantage as a means of control and gradually engages in a pattern of pulling away and coming back to shower her with apologies and love. This cycle is enough to sustain her but also painful enough that she becomes desperate to win him back each time he pulls away. He never fully leaves her in these dark times. Perhaps he just goes to a friend's house for a few nights. And he sends her text messages to string her along, assuring her that he is working to become a better husband and doesn't want to hurt her. She believes these things based on the faith that she has in the good sides of him that she has seen, heard, and felt, though these aspects seem to have faded.

We can see in this scenario that this pattern of behavior evolves and seems to form out of negative emotional experiences. Emotional pain is some of the hardest pain that humans have to deal with, and sometimes, people go to desperate measures to avoid it, even if it means hurting the ones we love in order to ensure that we don't lose them. This, of course, is not love. It is possessiveness and fear, and hopefully, Mandy realizes the type of toxic cycles that have formed out of her relationship and begins to seek help to get out of it.

Cults

The cult is an interesting topic because there are often lots of different manipulative and dark psychology techniques going on at the same time. Once a person has been hooked through some kind of promise of emotional or spiritual fulfillment, the human mind often works against itself in the way illustrated above when the object of desire is something we want so badly that we ignore red flags going up in our minds about the situations we've gotten ourselves into. When we are desperate to believe in something or someone, there are no limits to how deep we can bury our heads into the sand in order to give ourselves the illusion that we are living the way that we want and getting what we want out of this lifestyle. This has been the case for many people who have come forward years after having been sucked into a cult that was found to be practicing very unsavory things behind the curtain, including child abuse and other forms of sexual abuse, verbal abuse, torture, etc. Even those who may have seen these behaviors going on were sometimes too buried in the mire of the cult's beliefs and under so much influence that they were able to turn a blind eye and convince themselves that there was nothing really immoral going on.

This should ring a bell in relation to the psychological experiments we talked about earlier in which people were able to convince themselves that the higher-ups and people in control knew better, and what they were doing was completely sanctioned by "smarter" people with nothing but good intentions. The Milgram experiment illuminated this aspect of human psychology quite clearly and in a fascinating way. It often held up a light to understand a little bit better how a malicious movement like the fascist party could have risen to power under such seemingly immoral conduct and motivations. The human mind is a powerful and complex mechanism, and the power of social influence should never be underestimated.

Chapter 6: Dark Psychology and Seduction

Dark Psychology in the realm of seduction is our next topic, and one which has caused a large amount of heartbreak, trauma, and tragedy for countless men and women. But the application of dark psychology when it comes to seduction and the romantic world is, again, part of a spectrum of tactics, not all of which are overtly malicious.

Someone who enters the dating world and presents only the best sides of himself is practicing a form of dark psychology in that he is presenting a sort of "white lie" as he hides the things about himself that he thinks a woman may not like or may prompt negative judge about him without first getting to know him. We are all guilty of making false, negative assumptions about people sometimes before we even talk to them, so a degree of this is totally understandable. But when the lie persists, and there is never a fully open two-way exchange of trust and respect, then there is fertile ground for turmoil and even abuse.

In this chapter, we will be discussing the more malicious applications of dark psychology within the realm of seduction.

One of the most dangerous things about the practice of dark psychology in romantic relationships is that not only can the effects be devastating and have long-lasting effects, but the perpetrator also often carries out these insidious strategies over a long time while distorting and playing with the target's emotions. When a person has successfully gained the trust of another individual, that person becomes very vulnerable in the realm of emotions because trusting someone means believing in positive motivations and good decision-making even when you don't have all the facts or do not have a front-row seat to what's going on.

For example, if a married woman finds out her husband is going on a trip for work, she may or may not feel uneasy about the situation. If the relationship has a healthy amount of trust and respect without any prior infractions, then it is likely the woman will not feel too much anxiety about the prospect of her husband going away for a few days, much less the idea that he is going to cheat on her with a coworker. If the husband has that intention, then having established trust beforehand ensures that he is likely to get away with his intentions without worrying about his wife having the slightest suspicions. But, chances are, a man who just wants to sleep around is not going to go through the trouble of establishing a stable marriage for years before enacting his plans. And it would be difficult for this man to convince his wife of a completely different persona for that period of time, and the effort would not be worth it unless there were additional hidden goals motivating those efforts. A man who goes through this much work to establish a different persona from his own for the sake of self-betterment and advantage ventures into the realm of the dark triad persona set, which we will get deeper into in the next chapter.

For the purposes of this chapter, we will focus on the seduction that takes place at the very beginning of a relationship. As mentioned previously, the use of dark psychology may not be a focused, conscious effort, but simply some advice a person got from a friend or something he read online on a dating forum. For whatever reason, the dark psychology practitioner in this scenario will begin with some careful observation and information gathering before making his first move. Just as in the prior example of an individual trying to take over a room and become an alpha-like presence in the room, someone with a singular target whom he wishes to win over within as little as a few minutes will begin by making sure he's chosen the best target for his intentions. It's not enough to just pick out someone whom he finds attractive. He must also look out for additional signs that this woman is going to be open to an approach at all, let alone a friendly conversation. The setting itself could be just about anywhere that it would be appropriate to approach someone you don't know and introduce yourself. The environment may be a place like a party or a bar or some other public place where people hang out regularly. But we could also be talking about a quiet coffee shop, a park, or outside a bus stop. People meet acquaintances in all kinds of places, and, once the target is chosen, the place where the practitioner will want to make his first move must be a place where it is going to be comfortable and convenient to carry out a conversation. For example, he wouldn't want to meet his target while she's busy on her way to work or obviously trying to accomplish a task that demands her full attention. Rather, he wants to catch her somewhere where she is relaxed and just enjoying something without a lot of stress involved. People in this environment and state of mind will be more open to unplanned meetings and events, and he will want his target to be as comfortable and open as possible.

One of the most important decisions that the practitioner will make when using dark psychology in seduction is choosing the target. We often watch programs or news reports of someone being abducted or fooled into doing something a person didn't want to do, and you might think, "I would never do that." Well, the truth is, most of us can be overconfident when it comes to making judgments and reading another person's character. Sometimes, we are correct, and other times, there is a very clever dark psychology user behind the scenes who only presents what he wants us to believe in on the outside.

The target will often be young and exude personality traits that are consistent with someone who is open and friendly and likely to engage with a stranger. In this example, we are looking at the dark psychology user who is planning to approach a complete stranger in a public place with the hopes that he can develop some kind of connection that will open the door to more interactions. You might think that one of the key ingredients to a plan like this is that the practitioner has to be really attractive. But the truth is that men can impress and charm other people without necessarily being the most attractive man in the room. If he's got the right preparations and knowledge in place, a man can be very charming without being devastatingly handsome, though this factor would certainly not hurt.

Different women are attracted to different types of personalities, and the practitioner who is aiming to charm a woman must pick up on these desired traits rather quickly into the interaction or personify them based on information he has gathered about her past and what type of men she likes. Keep in mind that the tables can easily be turned here where we are talking about a woman who is using dark psychology to seduce a man, though the tactics there will work in a woman's favor as the guide to most men's immediate attraction is purely physical. A man looking to seduce a woman can be a little trickier, so this is why we are looking at the process from this angle.

First impressions involve what most people view as superficial aspects of a person. When the man approaches his target, he will be dressed in a way that conveys to the target what he wants her to see. Is he a busy professional who was stopped in his tracks and just had to say hello? If so, he might be wearing a business casual ensemble with some pricey-looking accessories. Perhaps he is a sporty type and is wearing something casual but made to move in. This could be the route he would take if he wanted to catch while she was out for a job or a long walk. Perhaps he wants to look younger and adopts more of a gently tussled, boho kind of style to mirror the target's style, etc. His appearance will play into this first encounter and the impression he makes on his target, but then he has to open his mouth.

His approach is careful to be non-threatening and casual. He doesn't want to scare her away by approaching her with an obvious objective, say, of spouting off a pickup line then asking for a phone number. The best approach will happen if it appears the man just happens to be in the same place at the same time and is intrigued by the appearance of this attractive woman. He doesn't want to assume to steal away her time if she is not amenable to giving it away, and the approach itself might have to wait until a better time if he does not get a positive response right away. If it appears he is bothering her in any way, he will probably need to take a step back and try again another time, or else move on to a different target.

But if he is successful and approaches in a way that does not alarm the target, she will send him a positive signal, such as a smile or a greeting. The progression to seduction will depend a lot on how well the dark psychology practitioner reads the target and how well he responds in a way that is effective and positively reinforcing his selected persona. Those who are skilled in this area will be able to charm the woman rather quickly. He knows that women like to be listened to and to feel like the person cares about what she is saying. To play into this, the practitioner may throw all kinds of wonderful compliments and questions and interest at her in order to convey that he is not only listening but very interested in everything she has to say. This will create a sense of camaraderie, and the longer this can be maintained, the more the target will feel comfortable talking,

and eventually, she might even release details about her life that will further work toward the practitioner's goals.

What the user will look for in this situation are the little subtle cues that the target is interested in. Often, we, as human beings, give signals subconsciously without our immediate awareness, and we all have certain reactions that go off automatically when we are entertained or interested in a conversation. The more positive signals the target gives off, the more these are taken by the dark psychology practitioner as a go-ahead to move forward with the interaction and to turn on the charm as much as possible.

The goal of this first interaction is to secure a second interaction. This could be explicit with an outright invitation to hang out again in the future or for a date, or it could be another "coincidental" meeting at which both of these individuals run into each other, perhaps during a similar activity or set of circumstances as this first interaction. Each time the practitioner interacts with his target, the goal will be to increase the attraction that may have started when the two of them first met. The progression will look a lot like a dating situation, but the dark psychology user is using tactics that are covering up the truth of the motivations and goals underneath.

In another scenario, the practitioner may have the goal to get a girl to come home with him the same night. One of the most commonly used tools in this scenario is alcohol, with the intent of getting a girl drunk enough that she begins to make poor decisions and  become overly trusting of complete strangers. When this situation is created, the dark psychology practitioner can simply make a few suggestions, and the woman may be convinced that she is in safe hands and can trust this man for a fun night without any commitments afterward.

Women can protect themselves from predatory behavior by being aware of the common tactics and warning signs when engaging with strangers. Some of the advice you've heard for years seem trite and obvious until a woman finds herself in a situation where her senses and thinking are clouded or distracted. It is also important to be on guard and aware of situations that may arise with close friends or family. Friends who attend a big party or go to a bar together should never abandon the group in favor of spending time with a man whom she just met that night, especially if she is drinking. Her friends should not allow this to happen, even if she insists, as the man in question seems unbelievably charming. The old saying about things that seem too good to be true usually are, is told over and over for a reason. If you suspect that someone you care about is under the influence of a master manipulator, it is important to talk with them about the possibility that they are being lied to as a means of getting something in return but not being straightforward. Don't be afraid to start that conversation if you believe there is a possibility that someone you care about is in danger. A lot of people may find the idea intimidating, or they hesitate because the friend might think they are overbearing or overstepping their bounds. It is always better to find yourself in disagreement with a friend than to find out that he or she has been abused or mistreated by someone they had thought they could trust or developed feelings for.

The truth is, when a practitioner of dark psychology is able to get past the seduction phase successfully, they will often continue the ruse because they enjoy playing with the control and trust they've won and enjoy basking in their prize. They may be using the individual as a way to make themselves look good, like a trophy, or they may be using this person as a means to some other end. The motivations behind such manipulation and abuse can vary widely, and the damage that can be done in the end should never be underestimated.

Chapter 7: The Dark Triad

The dark triad involves a set of deviant personalities, which are known very commonly to employ tactics of dark psychology as a regular, routine practice in their interactions with people. This is because what we consider normal interactive abilities and social skills are different in some way in regard to these three personality types, if they are there at all. The social skills set often developed by these personality types center around manipulation and the pretense of being normal and conveying normal human emotions. They find out very soon that this is absolutely necessary because they do not have the capacity for these particular feelings toward others. We often cite people in these three categories as being without feeling or without empathy for others. This means that they do not feel bad about hurting others or their pain when they are sad. They do not even feel empathy toward another person's feelings of anger and frustration. The members of this circle remain enigmas in a lot of respects, mostly because it is difficult for someone who is not a part of this circle to understand how someone could possibly function in a way that is devoid of human empathy and caring or true, honest love. These three personalities of the dark triad include the sociopath, the narcissist, and the Machiavellian personality type. We will take a look at each of these categories in more detail.

Sociopath

The sociopath is often confused with another category of deviant personalities, the psychopath. However, they are different in a few key ways.

The most commonly recognized difference between the sociopath and the psychopath is that the sociopath personality is developed after birth, while the psychopath is born with this particular deformity. Sociopaths endure experiences such as childhood trauma or abuse, or perhaps they learn non-empathy from role models or the people with whom they are brought up around. Whatever the examples, this behavior pattern and mindset are developed or learned through a process of living and experiences that involve triggers and formulations for the deviant personality type, while the psychopath is innate in the affected person at birth, including all that this personality involves. The sociopath and the psychopath can be very similar in nearly every other way that people are commonly familiar with. But the fact that the sociopathic personality is formed as a result of living and learned through experiences means that there is a lot of room for subtle changes and emotional nuance. The sociopath is not immune to

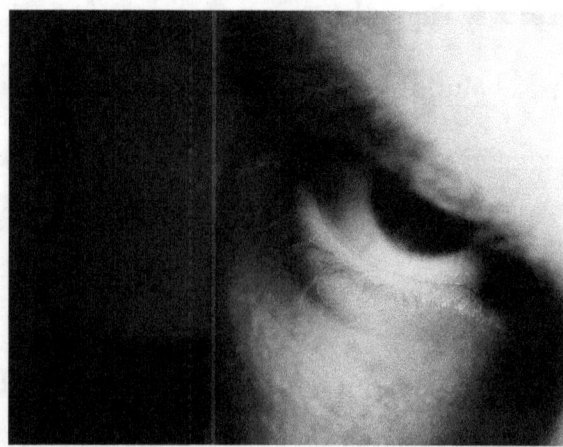

feelings like empathy and guilt, though the threshold is quite high, and these feelings might be ignored in favor of continuing the hurtful behavior simply because the sociopath still places himself higher in importance above other people. The psychopath, on the other hand, did not develop feelings of empathy or pick up on subtle changes in emotions through experience and learned behavior. They are simply not wired with the capacity to feel for others.

Sociopaths often develop skills related to dark psychology strategy out of the necessity to convince other people around them that they are "normal" in the sense of human compassion, empathy, romantic love, etc. To do this, they figure out what makes people tick and how to fool people. This develops in many different ways. Perhaps they had an adult figure at a young age who taught them through example how to lie and cheat and manipulate to get what they want. Perhaps they started to try things on a trial-and-error basis to figure out what works and what doesn't with different sorts of people. Or, perhaps they grabbed a few books and did some practical studying to understand the human brain and the psychology of emotions. However, they eventually get to a place where they have mastered some dark psychology skills, and they usually end up using people on a regular basis in their adult lives simply out of habit and necessity to continue living for the benefit of themselves.

Narcissist

The term narcissist is probably thrown around even more often than sociopath and psychopath and comes with its own set of connotations. The narcissist is often depicted as the well-dressed man with a deceptive smile and "affect" who goes around fooling people into doing things for him or giving him things under false pretenses. These "gifts" can be anything from money and donations to sex, power, influence, and admiration. The narcissist has an addiction to satisfying himself and his own needs and desires. He pursues fame and appreciation and

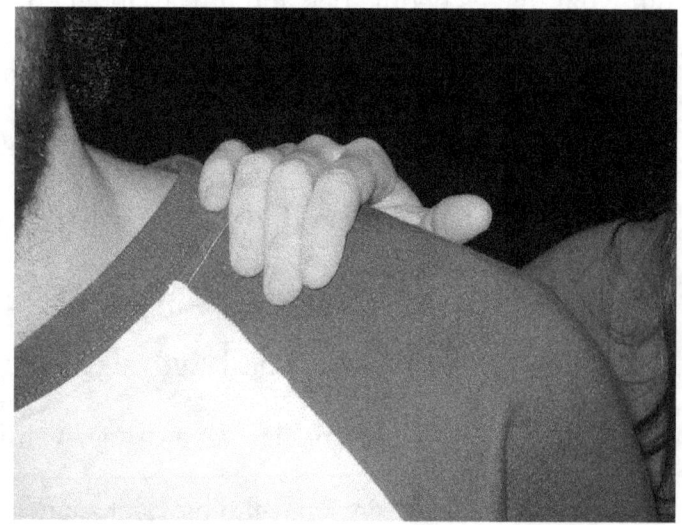

praise and will do whatever is necessary to place himself above everyone else and then to gloat about it. The narcissist is also devoid of human emotions where it concerns other people. He does not love in a conventional way; he simply pretends to love another for the sake of being loved in return. It is all about him.

Narcissists develop as a response to life experience, how he is raised, or how he is treated by others. The narcissist is not born a narcissist like a psychopath is born a psychopath. However, while the sociopath may be able to recover some capacity for empathy, guilt, and compassion, it is rarely seen that a narcissist makes any degree of the same kind of recovery. In other words, once a narcissist, always a narcissist. Now, the narcissist may be very clever in that he could convince persons of interest that he has changed or seen the light or "come to Jesus" in this respect, but it is, most often, a complete lie in order to get some type of attention or praise. Again, manipulation and dark psychology are the narcissist's bread and butter, and when those skills start to develop, and the individual sees the fruits of his labor, it only gives the narcissist more fuel and motivation to continue and get better at these skills. They will use the skills on anybody and often target those who are emotionally vulnerable and naïve.

We talked earlier about the "long game" in which a practitioner of dark psychology invests months, years, and even decades into manipulating and controlling a single individual. This is most often associated with a spouse, partner, or business colleague. The possibilities here are countless in terms of what exactly the narcissist is aiming for, but we can be assured that it is something about personal gain in some form.

The tragedy among those who are fooled into believing a narcissist is someone he isn't is that the target who has fallen in love often falls into the trap of believing they can somehow "change" the narcissist through enough love and dedication. This is especially sad because it feeds perfectly into the narcissist's trap who only desires to keep the claws of attachment deeply ingrained in his target so that he can continue to siphon love, support, and affirmations for as long he wants. We discussed earlier a technique in which the target is strung along then pushed away, only to be brought back together and given satisfaction until the next time the practitioner pulls away. This technique cultivates a feeling of desperation in the target with just enough attention and occasional showers of affection that the target does not cut ties completely. This is an ideal situation for the narcissist who desires to pursue other interests without having to dedicate all of his energies on a single target. He may utilize an occasional form of communication in order to make sure his first target is still "waiting" on him while he very well could be exercising a whole new romantic situation with another vulnerable female.

The narcissist gets a lot of excitement and satisfaction from challenging himself and finding himself successful in manipulating those "hard to get" types. It is just another source for him to glean self-praise and admiration. He will also move against anyone else in his purview who tries to usurp what he has gained or exposes him to other people. He will also use any measures necessary to accomplish the removal of those obstacles. The great majority of serial killers fall under the category of the narcissist, among others, as they are obviously willing to do whatever needs to be done in order to satisfy their own desires. They do not feel guilt or shame in the same way that "neurotypical" human beings do, or else this sensation would override their desires, though they often insist, once caught, that they had felt remorse after killing.

Machiavellian

This component of dark triad personalities is named after an individual who espoused a work called *The Prince* that states that the necessity for proper and effective leadership is absolute in the sense that, essentially, "the ends justify the means." The leader must do what is necessary in order to enforce rules and maintain power. Nothing is off the table when it comes to making sure these needs are met and to eradicate any threat to that seat of power. His writings supported the use of force, fear, and harsh punishment as a means of making sure the populace remained under control and were discouraged from going against the leader's wishes and orders.

The Machiavellian personality is most closely associated with the personal accumulation of wealth. He is the miser sitting atop his mountain of gold while  looking around at everyone else who lives without sufficient means even to live. He is also without much capacity to feel for other human beings. He does not look at the less fortunate and feel compelled to give some of his wealth; he is more likely to look at the penny or two in their possession and try to take them for himself.

Dark Psychology Tactics of the Dark Triad

The three components of the dark triad are centers for demonstrating the necessity to manipulate and use dark psychology tactics as a way to function in a world full of people who are different from you in a few very important ways. The lack of that which makes us feel like we can connect and use other people as support mechanisms for getting through life necessitates that those needs are fulfilled elsewhere. What exactly is it that the narcissist lives for, if not to connect with others or have a family to nurture and protect? The answer for all three of these personality types is that the self becomes a god at an early age, and everything the individuals do thereafter is, in effect, an act of worship to that god.

To illustrate, think of a devoutly religious follower who devotes a good amount of time to the study and worship of that god. Everything this believer does is pursued through the lens of doing what his god wants, and he follows the rules and regulations set before him in ancient religious texts as a sort of guide for how he is to live his life. If he feels called to go to a foreign country as part of a missionary trip, then he will do what he can to raise the money to support himself while he is away and take every opportunity to do what needs to be done there in the name of his god.

The personalities of the dark triad function in a similar way, only in that they themselves are the gods who they follow and worship. When a god calls for sacrifice, even if the sacrifice is another human being, history has shown that human beings are willing to offer this blood for the sake of satiating the desires of their gods. The narcissist, too, will sacrifice other people in the name of what is more important and the person in his life who is most deserving above all others—himself. The same line of thinking follows for the other components of the dark triad, each centering on his own specific obsessions and pursuits, none of them altruistic in nature but completely self-serving.

The problem for them is that to get what they want, they often need to go through other people. And this is where the necessity for dark psychology comes in. Not only will they often have a natural affinity for the skill, but they also find it fun to mess with people. They feel affirmed to look as if they have made a fool of others, which props themselves up as the smarter, superior being. They themselves would never consider that they could be susceptible to such manipulation, and

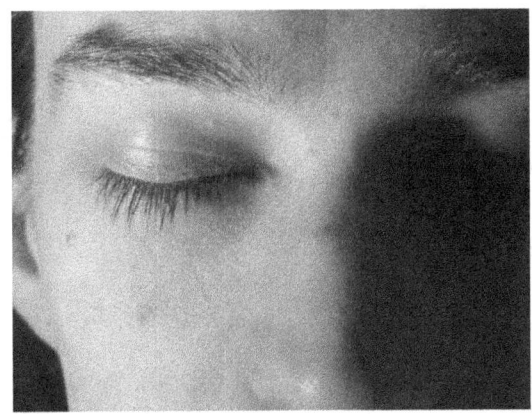

they are often immune to such strategies for the simple fact that they don't have those pesky emotional vulnerabilities that most other people share. They do not trust others but instead seek to get other people to trust them, love them, and admire them.

The easiest way to fool others in this regard is to closely observe and then emulate human behaviors that will make them appear as though they feel just as other people feel. They can make people fall in love with them, or they might exploit another's pity through deception in order to get a handout or some other type of free influence—whatever needs to be done.

One of the most fascinating and insidious characteristics of the members of the dark triad personality group is their capacity for denial when it comes to being challenged directly when they are caught in their schemes. In terms of gaslighting practices, when they are given clear evidence of their behavior and are asked to acknowledge their actions, they will simply disregard and deny without budging an inch. This is infinitely frustrating for the victims or the individuals trying to make sense of the dark triad's motivations and foundations for behavior. All we can do is stare at them in awe of how they can so readily disregard any and all attention to others and their concerns simply because they don't care; perhaps they are even bored.

The most painful experience in relation to dealing with individuals of the dark triad personality types is when that realization comes through, and you are unable to completely get rid of the feelings you've developed for this mask that has been hiding an insidious person. When the realization hits the victim, it is like having that person with whom they've been in a relationship suddenly disappear. It can feel as if the love of one's life has died, and there is just this demon in his/her place. If the target cannot come to terms with this realization and this unmasking of the truth, then she may try for years and years to get back that illusion of a relationship, even going so far as to live in denial herself. This is one of the most truly tragic results that can occur in a situation involving dark triad personalities and dark psychology.

But there are even more horrible ends to a situation in which a dark triad personality pursues a desire and stops at nothing to gain it. Murder, abuse, and other inconceivably horrible actions have been utilized in order to satisfy the simple, basic urges within them. That part of most of us which will stop us from doing such things for the sake of selfish pursuits is completely absent in these individuals, and their most basic urges and selfish desires often have free reign and influence over their behavior. It is a terrifyingly fascinating structure within these individuals that they can at once be harboring such animalistic and selfish natures while being perceived by other people as persons of high moral standing and poise. These traits make those on the spectrum of the dark triad personalities some of the most dangerous people on the planet.

Chapter 8: The Art of Deception and Mind Games

Harry Houdini was a famous entertainer and escape artist who mastered his craft at an early age and became known around the world at the turn of the 20th century for his risky public escapes and meeting challenges presented to him while a crowd of onlookers watched in amazement. Newspapers would advertise where he would be and what he was planning to do so that when he was ready to perform his stunts, there would be a massive crowd of people waiting for him. Most people today who recognize his name immediately associate him with the amazing escapes he performed, such as getting out of a straight jacket or escaping from chains while submerged underwater. What many don't know is that in the latter part of his career, he also became obsessed with the occult and the idea that one could talk to those who had passed away through rituals known as "seances." But he soon became angry about the appearance of scam artists whom he claimed were taking people's money and then faking the ritual through the use of cheap tricks that make customers believe they were actually reaching dead loved ones and relatives. It angered him so much that he took it upon himself to attend some of these events and expose the tricksters, catching them in the act, as he was familiar with the tricks they would use because he was an accomplished and well-studied magician who could spot what was going on. The routine would go something like this:

Houdini would attend one of these seances under the guise of having lost someone he loved. He would play the part well of a grieving husband and make up a story to support his claims. He would then sit down at a large table with other guests who were also there to try and communicate with lost loved ones. The seance would progress with a selection of tricks and techniques which would transform the atmosphere and play with the guests' perceptions of what was happening. Houdini would be able to spot these things, ranging from rigged lights and surfaces that would move on command or emit light seemingly from nowhere. Eerie sounds would float through the air, and the guests were told that it was the arrival of spirits, but Houdini knew that there were other people involved who were putting these things into action under the cover of dimmed lights, etc. He would stand up and abruptly interrupt the proceedings in order to expose what was going on. These events and Houdini's actions would be told through news stories, and he soon became well-known for his personal mission to expose frauds in this way. An interesting detail is that Houdini did actually believe in communication with those who had passed into the afterlife. He even talked with his wife about a secret phrase he would use should one of them pass so that they could communicate when one would try to reach the other. After Houdini died tragically following a stage performance, his wife tried for years and years to reach her husband using this secret phrase and utilizing every medium she could find, to no avail.

This example of the rigged seance is brought up here as a good illustration of how mind games can work together to form a completely altered reality in the minds of the victims. Let's begin with an examination of the target's initial mindset.

The seance practice targeted those individuals who had lost a loved one and wished desperately to communicate with them. They would have been in varying stages of the grief process, and anyone would pinpoint these individuals as being emotionally vulnerable. The intensity of certain emotions can drive human beings to do crazy things and to experience even more outlandish ideas and  thought processes. The human mind actually has an incredible capacity and proclivity to do what it can to protect itself from pain, including emotional pain. When we get close to something hot, and we are in danger of being burned, our nerves send a signal to our brains in the form of increased pain as we get closer to the source. This tells us to get away from that source of danger immediately, and we often react physically even before our minds process what is going on. Anyone who has ever accidentally touched something burning hot can attest to this phenomenon.

We also have built-in mechanisms which are triggered when we are dealing with emotional pain. Depending on the intensity of emotions, the mind can trick us into believing something that isn't true—this is the case in those situations where someone is given tragic news, and their initial reaction is denial until they can wrap their minds around what is happening. We may also be prone to reaching out to far-fetched possibilities in the hopes of easing the intensity of the pain, which comes with loss, even so far as, say, reaching out to someone who promises that they can connect us with those lost loved ones.

The first use of dark psychology tactics appears in the form of the salesman who speaks to a potential customer—someone hurting emotionally as a result of a terrible loss. Here, the salesman listens intently with a sympathetic ear. He hears everything that the subject says and relays his feelings of empathy and condolences. This step is incredibly important for the manipulator because this is when he will begin to glean details and information that he will need to use later to support his ruse. He will listen to little details specific to the lost loved one. This tactic was often used as a way to personalize the experience and heighten the sense of believability during the seances themselves. He may pick up during this initial conversation that the customer's daughter was killed during a train accident, for example. She had been traveling with a pet dog and was wearing one of her favorite blue dresses, etc. People who are in the middle of a grieving process or who are going through some other type of emotional distress might be inclined to ramble as a way to relive and touch those experiences and those people who no longer exist in their lives. Talking about lost loved ones has a way of reinvigorating their memory and, in a way, brings them to life for a brief time as those memories are alive in the subject's mind and heart while she speaks. The target may not even realize that she is relinquishing these details but may be lost in reverie, to the dark psychology user's benefit.

The customers might then be brought into a specially prepared room. One of the key aspects of this deception is the ambiance of the room itself. The room would have been dimly lit, with a large table as the focus of the room. The individual who is supposed to be the conduit for the spirits to use for communication may wear a special outfit or something that signifies that they are a special component in this exercise. The room may be outfitted with lots of candles to enhance the otherworldly feeling of the environment and the customers' intentions.

The customers all sit down at the table, usually a big circle, and then the next very important step to the ritual begins. The leader of the ritual speaks to the customers in an urgent, sincere tone that signifies the beginning of a very sacred and intense proceeding. The speaker uses aspects of character, such as tone of voice, eye contact, and intensity, to convey the weight of what is about to happen. As the targets listen to this proceeding, they begin to feel the passing of intensity, and this further heightens the environment's otherworldly effect. The mind does the rest in terms of solidifying that the targets are being thoroughly convinced of their situation and what is about to happen. Each subject is desperate for this situation to be real, and they do well in convincing themselves through hopes and wishes that they will soon be able to connect with those they desperately miss. At this point, their own minds are working against them in the form of denial as they dismiss any rational argument that may be trying to enter their minds regarding the validity of what they are experiencing. They make the decision to trust what these people are saying, and, once this happens, the door opens wide for continued deception and mind games.

The next step in the proceeding is for the actual ritual to begin. Effects designed to startle and amaze the targets are put into action according to a meticulously laid out plan. Things start to happen, which appear to be happening without anyone in the room having any influence on those actions. These would include things like candles being blown out, the table moving or rumbling objects placed on the table moving without anyone's volition, and other similar actions. Noises and eerie sounds that were designed to sound like they are coming from the beyond would also emanate at key points in the ritual's proceedings. As these phenomena happen, the subjects would be fed further proof that what they are experiencing is real as they continue to take what they are indeed real and valid. The mind processes only those things which prop up and substantiate what it has already decided to believe. At the same time, those minds would have immediately disregarded evidence that pointed to the contrary belief that all this was a ruse. For example, if someone were to accidentally step out of the shadows and into the customer's view from the table, the customer, having already solidified himself in his beliefs about the proceedings, would likely not even process that person's presence in their visual field.

Another common practice that served to help make the deceptions and tricks so convincing was to have the subjects hold each other's hands in clear view of each other, including the leader of the seance ritual. Doing this was evidence that these strange phenomena were not being enacted or influenced in any way by the ritual leader, so, as logic could enter the picture in these subjects' grieving and desperate minds, the only presence that could be enacting these phenomena were those present in the afterlife coming to talk to them.

The next component of the ritual lies in the acting skills of the ritual leader. She was presented as one through which the subjects' loved ones could reach out and speak to them. The level of the suspension of disbelief here is a vivid and potent reminder of how much our own minds can play a part in the deceptive mind games involved in dark psychology.

And this is where that information, gleaned earlier from each of the subjects, would come into play. The actor might start to act strangely, and she would completely change the tone and timbre of her voice in order to convey that she was being "taken over" by the spirits in the room. The actor would then begin addressing each subject under the guise of their lost loved ones. This might be played up as if the subject's loved ones were actively searching for the presence of their family or friend. The subject might then be prompted to reach out and say something like, "I'm here. I'm listening." The subjects would then be able to have brief conversations, and perhaps the actor would describe how the connection was a little cloudy, and she could only relay a few sentiments to their loved ones of their choosing. The actor might also say a few words through an altered voice that was meant to be believed as the voice of the lost loved one. Imagine being one of these poor people believing they were talking to their dead loved ones. The experience must have been mind-altering, and the impressions on the ritual would have lasted for a long time afterward, perhaps being one of the few things the subjects would cling to as sustenance for years to come.

The ritual would conclude according to a planned timeline of events. The subjects would not be allowed to simply say everything they wanted to or to have an hours-long conversation with their dead loved ones because the longer the ruse goes on, the higher the likelihood that something is going to trip the scammers up, or the customer might venture into unknown territory that they would not be able to play into. After the final escalation of the ritual, the mood and intensity are gradually brought down, as the spirits essentially "go back" to where they had come from, and the original demeanor and voice returns to the ritual leader. They dispel the illusion and are brought back to reality and left to ponder what has just happened to them. In the scammer's idea of a best-case scenario, the customers would come back, again and again, to speak to their loved ones, forming a continuous line of income that is graciously accepted.

Cold Reading

Cold reading refers to a dark psychology tactic that exploits a similar facet of human nature, which is the desire to believe what we want to believe and also to see patterns and connections where we desire to see them. Research has uncovered a tendency in human nature to personalize the information that actually applies to a broad spectrum of people. This is illustrated most clearly in the horoscope that you find online or used to find in newspapers, where there was a set of "readings" that people would apply to themselves based on their birthdays. The horoscopes would be written out for each individual month of the year and corresponded with each month's astrological sign. These "messages" and readings can be fascinating to people who are particularly susceptible to this phenomenological tendency to associate themselves with personal readings like this, which are, in fact, broadly applicable. If you go through and read not just your own month's readings but all of them, you would find that a lot of the other readings also find meaning in connection to your own life, simply because of the broad possibilities of interpretation and application present.

Cold readings follow the same principle and are generally applied in face-to-face interactions; only, the process in this situation is a progression rather than a static series of statements such as in a horoscope.

The cold reading begins with broad generalizes statements and progresses to individual personalization based on the subject's reactions. These reactions are relayed with not only words themselves but also with body language and micro-expressions or expressions that are so brief and minute that most people don't pick up on them unless someone is really looking for them. The practiced cold reader is one of these people and knows what to look for. These signals are important to notice because they will give the practitioner clues as to whether or not he is heading in the right direction. A negative micro-expression might signal that he is off and needs to switch gears, while a positive signal will tell him to keep going along the same track. Some of this is navigated through a series of questions in the form of trial and error. A tidbit of information is followed until the trail runs cold, and the reader must try something different.

Positive expressions and signals include things like wide-eyed expressions of amazement or of being startled, signifying that the reader has hit on a truth that the subject is surprised he knows about. Grinning and chuckling can be other positive tells in this context. Body language also plays a big role in cueing the reader on whether he is heading in the right direction or not, and we will discuss this facet in more detail in chapter 10.

As an example, let's examine the following conversation.

The subject is greeted and is smiling and excited about the prospect of cold reading. She might be a little skeptical, but she also thinks it is fun to try out. The reader will recognize this as a good subject simply because there is eagerness as well as a limited level of skepticism. She isn't completely against the idea that someone could cold read her, and this is the type of attitude that makes a good cold reading subject.

The reader might start with some broad statements and assumptions based on the subject's current mood and demeanor. "You've been having a pretty good day today." The subject smiles and giggles. "And you've been able to share some good times with people you love." More smiles, more positive reinforcement. "You've got a special someone here with you today." The subject looks suddenly embarrassed, signaling he's hit the jackpot. "Ah, maybe this person doesn't even realize he is the subject of your affections." At this point, there might be a reaction from someone in the crowd. From the surface, it seems as though the reader has simply read this female without her giving him any information. But the truth is, she has given him a great deal of information, even if she wasn't aware of it. This is the nature of dark psychology.

Chapter 9: What Is Brainwashing?

The term brainwashing has a long and interesting history of connotations and associations. Sometimes, the first thing people might think of is the appearance of brainwashing and mentions of the process in movies and TV, in which hyper-evil individuals use psychological and sometimes, super-human techniques to get another person or group of people to do their bidding. Much like the

misconception of hypnosis as a way to turn people into robots, the idea that brainwashing is a process by which a person can be turned into a robot for use by some dominant entity is also false and grossly exaggerated.

Brainwashing refers to the manipulation of the mind through dark psychological strategies and fits snugly under the umbrella of several topics that we have already discussed. Tactics, such as gaslighting and cult-recruitment, all employ a level of brainwashing and varying degrees and forms of dark psychology. During the era of the Milgram experiment, researchers and the curious used the term to examine the phenomenon of a collection of seemingly intelligent and "normal" people who could enact such atrocities as was witnessed during the holocaust.

At the core of the brainwashing process is consistent repetition. We've discussed the process of gaslighting and how this effect manifests over time as the same untruths and deceptions are repeated and reinforced many times over a period of time. Brainwashing, too, takes time, as well as repetition and consistent reinforcement as a way to condition the brain either away from old habits or to form new ones in the way of new belief systems and paradigms. We can look at the Jonestown cult phenomenon as a good example of how this is done and can be done.

Jim Jones was an incredibly charismatic speaker. He was skilled with communicating with people, and he could impress upon them that he could lead them to a place of salvation and refuge from their pain and suffering, which took on as many forms as there were followers. His words were powerful, but he also used additional tactics to further cement his followers' belief in him through things like rigged "miracle" healings. This might sound familiar from our discussion of seances and the tactics used by scammers to solidify the witnesses' suspension of disbelief. Those who fell into the cult's mindset and belief system were also taken advantage of by recruiters playing on the individuals' fears, emotions, desires, and sources of pain. The promise of a way out of suffering is something that all of us have the capacity to be tempted by. And those of us who think we would be above such tactics, and would never buy into such ideas from a cult, could possibly have been prime targets for these recruiters simply based on their willful ignorance. No one is completely above human psychology, and all of us have emotions and pain that occupy our time and energy in an effort to find ways to alleviate those sources of suffering.

The point at which a potential victim is convinced to hesitate is the moment when the brainwashing process begins. If a person is able to shut down an interaction completely without giving in an inch, it is likely that the perpetrator will simply move on to an easier target, and we will outline exactly how this can be done in our chapter on best practices and defenses. But if the initial approach is successful, then the recruiter or another type of brainwasher has managed to find a thread of connectivity that they can then build upon to form a more solid foundation inside the target's mindset. To enact a process of brainwashing on a freethinking individual, who is not a prisoner, is an indicator that the dark psychology practitioner has developed his skills and has planned the interaction down to that last detail, as it is often difficult to get complete strangers to let you in, to this degree. Most people have a healthy level of boundaries around them and their minds, but that is why hitting on vulnerability is vital to the successful brainwashing attempt. For example, the person out on the street looking for a victim to brainwash is certainly going to go for the young girl crying on a bench, as opposed to the happy-go-lucky jogger smiling and humming to a happy tune. There is a need present with the young girl, and if the brainwasher can find a way to convince her that he can assuage that need in some way, then there is an opportunity to begin that repetitive reinforcement until the girl believes whatever it is he wants her to believe.

We form habits and break habits all throughout our lives. Sometimes, we have to put forth a great deal of effort to break a bad habit. Other times, we simply form new ones without even trying, based on experience and the influence of others. The mind is malleable in the sense that a person intent on brainwashing another person for whatever reason can see progress as long as he is able to reinforce the ideas through repetition. All it takes is for the door to open just a crack. Then the progression is just a matter of time, unless something drastic happens and, for whatever reason, the interactions are cut short between brainwashing and the victim. These repetitions could entail things like the presentation of evidence or repeated arguments that are framed in such a way as to seem believable and well-founded. The process can become more efficient if more people are involved in the reinforcement process. In other  words, ten people arguing for the same beliefs is a lot more convincing than one lone person. When the brainwasher can employ more people into the ruse, then there is an element of peer pressure and the pressure to conform, which adds to the impact of the brainwashing process. This is something that certainly contributed to the followers' comfort level in the case of Jim Jones. The congregation of followers would regularly be surrounded by devout, passionate people, and the feeling in place must have been electrifying. Words spoken to the crowd in this context would have held a high level of intensity and an appearance of gravity unlike what they would have experienced should the words have been spoken on an individual level without the influence of others.

Chapter 10: The Importance of Body Language

Body language is one of the major components of many forms of dark psychology tactics. This is because body language is actually more prevalent in terms of communication between human beings than speech. The key is whether or not you know what to look for and how to interpret body language in various situations. Let's take a look at a few examples.

Body language is often discussed when we're talking about displays of power and dominance. We've talked about the use of dark psychology in efforts to take over a room as an alpha or to win over other people whom the practitioner wants to influence or establish rapport with. We have also talked about dark psychology in the context of dating and seduction, but in this chapter, we will take a deeper look at what is being said through nonverbal communication in these various situations.

Dominance

Body language is a key part of displaying dominance, no matter the context. When a person enters the room, people consciously and subconsciously make judgments about that person based on what they see, how they hold themselves, and other subtle cues of nonverbal communication.

Katie enters a room, and her head is held high. She is not staring at the floor; she is making eye contact with the people she passes by and offering a slight nod and a grin as a greeting. Her posture is erect, with her shoulder back, and her stride is wide and confident. There is a slight sway to her hips that seems natural, and her arms swing freely at her sides. She has yet to actually speak to anyone, but you can form a pretty clear picture of what this person looks like as she enters the room. What is her body language communicating to you?

If you can form some kind of picture based on this description, there should be several adjectives that might come to mind to describe her based on this nonverbal evidence. The first, as hinted at in the description, might be confidence. When someone holds themselves erect with their shoulders back, it tells people around her that she is not hiding from them and that she is confident enough to be on full display and to acknowledge and confront anyone she comes across, hence, the direct eye contact and brief greetings. And the higher the chin, the more the message moves across the confidence territory into the realm of dominance.

To assume and display dominance is to carry yourself in a way that does not connote fear or trepidation. The free swing of the arms and long strides suggests that she is not concerned with getting in anyone's way, and there is an unspoken expectation that people will get out of hers if need be.

Let us say Katie moves into one of the main offices, and there, she is awaited by a few powerful people who are meeting her for the first time. Now, we're ready for the handshake.

The handshake can actually say a lot more than most people know to look for, but it is common knowledge in the realm of power and money and politics that how you choose to shake someone's hand can be a strong signal to a person's attitude, as well as their perception of the person with whom they are shaking hands.

The way to signal a position of dominance involves shaking hands in a way that your hand is on top with the palm facing down. This places the other's hand in the subservient position or with the palm facing up. The grip and pressure which the person chooses to employ during a handshake also send a message about dominance. Politicians who are constantly being photographed as they shake hands with other leaders and political figures might make special efforts to convey dominance by shaking hands in this position and making sure their hand is sending a strong signal to those who know what it means.

Katie chooses, however, to shake hands in a balanced way that does not assume dominance but instead orients the position of hands as to be equal with palms facing each other. This sends a non-threatening message of balance and a willingness to cooperate with another. It is smart to avoid intimidating or using aggressive behaviors in a situation where you want to form a working relationship based on trust and mutual benefit. Katie also is careful to smile and directly address the people she is meeting with eye contact and attentiveness. This should echo back to the first instances in which we examined how attentiveness, listening, and active engagement with a speaker sends the signal that you are interested and invested in what the subject is saying.

From a broad point of view, we can say that Katie practices dominance and strong leadership when she is in front of her employees, and she likes to cultivate a balanced working relationship with higher-ups and colleagues of equal stature within the business.

There are certainly much more overt ways to assume dominance, such as outright aggression, and there are also very subtle, covert ways, such as in the instance of a young professional gradually taking over a room and winning the hearts of those whom he might later utilize to his advantage. The alpha then operates as

the individual on top until another comes along who wants to take the position for himself, and the alpha is challenged.

Seduction

Seduction is another major category in which body language plays an especially vital role, both on the part of the person trying to seduce and his subject.

The reading of body language comes into play in this scenario as soon as the seducer makes his approach. From the moment the target acknowledges the seducer, she begins sending signals, which are both conscious and subconscious messages that will either reinforce the efficacy of the seducer's tactics or give him warning signs that his target is not as open to suggestion as he'd thought at first. Let's look at some examples.

The seducer approaches from behind the subject, who may be standing and listening to some music about to begin at a bar. When the approach happens, the target must turn her body to orient herself to the speaker if she is acknowledging the approach and willingness to engage. The seducer then examines how much of her body begins orienting toward him and how much she is responding by keeping her orientation pointed away from the seducer. If she fully engages and turns to meet and look the seducer head-on, this is a strong signal that the lady is amenable to the interaction and is a strong positive sign that the seducer has chosen the right target for his intentions. On the other hand, if the target remains facing toward the stage and/or does not move to orient any part of her body toward the seducer, then she is sending a strong signal that she is completely uninterested in an interaction at that moment. This could be motivated by a variety of different reasons, but the seducer would usually abandon his approach and perhaps try again a little later; otherwise, he may simply move on to a different target entirely.

The seducer pays attention to every movement and mannerism the target makes as he is engaging with her. The trick for successful interaction and seduction, however, is not to appear as if he is trying so hard to read her thoughts through her behaviors and nonverbal communication. An attempt at seduction, for example, which is accompanied by lots of staring at the target's body instead of her face, is certainly not going to go over well, as the seducer's intentions are all but being broadcast by his behavior and areas of attention.

The skilled seducer will be able to multitask as he listens to the target's words and pays attention to nonverbal cues as much as possible, without seeming like this is what he's doing. The seducer must come off as comfortable, friendly, and nonthreatening. The idea is to ignite some kind of attraction in whatever form he can. Once this is accomplished, he can begin playfully moving in as he exploits this newfound weakness. Positive body language cues that will often signal to the seducer that he is progressing well include smiling and giggling while keeping the body oriented toward the seducer. Women who are simply pretending to be comfortable and engage will often smile and giggle playfully, but the orientation of their  bodies will give away their anxiety. The seducer would likely not move forward in this situation until he can inspire a little more comfort into the interaction. However, as the seducer persists, he also runs the risk of intensifying the anxiety, as the target may or may not be experiencing a gut instinct to stay away or get out of the situation. This can be a powerful tool on the part of the target if she is able to really pay attention and listen to her instincts when she feels something is a bit off.

As the seducer finds a target and is able to get some positive signals, he will use his own powers in the form of nonverbal communication to inspire attraction and interest. Flattery can be utilized in ways other than direct verbal communication. A seducer who wants to introduce just a bit of flirtation and sexual interest might let the target catch him looking briefly over her as he then quickly returns to face her. This tells her a lot of different things about the seducer, and if played correctly, it will work to the seducer's advantage if the signal comes off as playful and flirtatious without getting into creepy territory.

There is a balance to all of these behaviors and interactions, and the same methods may work differently based on the personality and demeanor of the target. This is why practiced seducers will zero in on specific types who more often respond positively to such advances.

Interest vs. Boredom

Sometimes, our body language broadcasts information about ourselves unintentionally, and this can be a fascinating thing to look for in public once you become familiar with some of the more common responses to human interaction.

Boredom is one of the things that can affect us in ways that we are unaware of until someone else points out directly the behavior or nonverbal message. Things like yawning almost subconsciously or eyes that wander off while someone is speaking are nonverbal communications that can tell a person that they're bored and uninterested in what you have to say. It can be quite embarrassing when a speaker knows what these signals mean and sees them going into action in the middle of a story or speech or monologue. Perhaps a perfect example of this happening is the high school classroom setting in which a room full of bored teenagers is leaning to the side with their heads in their hands. Sometimes, this  behavior is intentional and meant to convey the feeling of boredom, but oftentimes, these behaviors just happen as a response to the boredom before the individual even knows he's doing anything. For the practitioner of dark psychology tactics, being able to tell when what he is saying to a target is having an effect or not through the skill of interpreting body language can be essential to the success of the tactic. If he can't pick up on this, then the interaction will probably simply amount to a great deal of wasted time.

On the flipside, feigning interest is something that most of us are very capable of doing, and we have all likely practiced this kind of "white lie" in our lives at some point. We've all been at a party and had to listen to a person's story that was not particularly interesting, but you didn't want to be impolite, so you feigned interest. Can you think of some common nonverbal cues to signal to a person that you are interested in what they are saying?

The first one that most people think of, and which is probably the most important, is eye contact. Making eye contact while a person is speaking to you is one of the clearest ways you can convey interest and respect. If your eyes are wandering all over the place, the speaker is likely to pick up on the fact that he or she is not holding your interest. Smiling, nodding, and responding to questions while interjecting comments to reinforce that you are listening and processing what is being said are other common ways to relay that you are actively engaged in the interaction.

Chapter 11: Best Practices and Defenses

Now that you have a much clearer idea of the different types and practices of dark psychology practitioners, we'd like to provide you with a brief list of tips for you to incorporate into your arsenal. This would allow you to be always on guard should a situation arise in which you might be encountering dark psychology in your own life. Spread these tips around to the people who are close to you so that  you will not only help defend yourself but you will also protect those you care about and love. Erring on the side of caution is always preferable when finding yourself in a dangerous and confusing situation in which dark psychology is being used.

Trust Is a Commodity to Be Earned—Not Freely Given

Dark Psychology users often use the manipulation of emotions to bypass the guards we usually have up to help us discern between someone we can trust and someone we have no reason to trust yet. Yes, when someone who we don't know asks for help, it is often kind and generous to offer a helping hand, even if you don't know the person well. But there are certain situations when this behavior is inadvisable simply because of the possibility that the person asking for help does not have good intentions. One factor to pay attention to is the time of day or night when someone approaches you for help and whether or not the area is lit and in a public area. If you are out at night and there are no a lot of people around, then someone coming up to you and trying to get you to follow them somewhere should be a huge red flag. This person may be sincere, but he may also not be a good person. It would be preferable for you to feel safe and protect yourself by potentially leaving a person to deal with a flat tire on his car.

Don't Drink Alone

We're talking about being out at a party or at a bar as opposed to a nice glass of wine while you binge on Netflix at home. Never go out into a public setting alone where it would be easy for someone with bad intentions to take notice that you are alone and drinking. If you are somewhere waiting for company, be wary of anyone who tries to approach you and convince you to go somewhere while you are by yourself enjoying a drink.

Don't Be Afraid to Disengage

Most of us recognize that disengaging from interaction in the middle of a conversation is probably going to come off as pretty rude, but you should never discount a bad feeling about a situation just because you are afraid of being rude or impolite. Explain that you don't feel right about the interaction, or if you feel the need to do it, make up an excuse to get out of the situation quickly and leave. Call someone right away if you feel you need some backup or an escort home. If you are somewhere without a lot of people around, move toward a public area where there will be other people to ask for support if you feel the need.

Have a Panic Button

There are lots of gadgets and apps out there which offer discreet means of communicating with someone of your choosing should you find yourself in a situation you can't easily get out of without some help. If you are out by yourself for a walk or a jog or in a public place but are approached by someone who is a little aggressive in his tactics, you can simply press a button or open an app without the person noticing to let someone you trust know that you would like some help to get out of your situation. In today's modern world, it is highly advisable that you do your best not to be out and about without a way of communicating with people you trust in case anything comes up or happens unexpectedly.

Call Them Out

This defense may not be the most preferable for certain personalities, but for those of you who have no trouble speaking your mind and letting someone know when they are wasting your time, don't be afraid to call out a person who is trying to manipulate you and let them know you are on to their schemes. If the setting is public, go ahead and raise your voice a bit so that others can hear you. It may just serve as a warning to other potential targets in the area, and the practitioner will

likely feel embarrassed or feel the need to flee the scene, as his perfect cover has been blown.

Continue Your Study and Research of Dark Psychology Tactics

One of the best actions you can take as you guard yourself against future dark psychology tactics is to continue educating yourself on the myriad ways that dark psychology can manifest in day-to-day interactions and settings. These users are always trying to be creative, coming up with new and more insidious ways to get under people's skin for their own benefit and exploitation. The more you familiarize yourself with the possibilities, the better prepared you will be when a situation comes up.

Spread the Word

The knowledge and understanding you've gained from reading this book is something that could very well save you from a devastating situation in the future, which you would never see coming until it's too late. Letting others know about what you've learned and sharing the skills and tools explained in this book will serve to benefit others in the same way. If you know someone who has been the victim of dark psychology in some way, you know that this can have a devastating effect that often lasts for the rest of the victim's life. Emotional trauma and manipulation can be some of the most painful and insidious tactics a practitioner of dark psychology can use on another human being, so spending some time not only to educate yourself but also to educate others can be a really important way to save a person from this potential harm. Don't be afraid to talk to someone candidly if you feel there is someone in their life who is harming them in any of these ways. The human mind can often deceive itself through denial, and sometimes, it takes input from another rational mind to bring these individuals out of this dark place. It's worth the risk of being called nosy when you are legitimately afraid for another person's safety, especially if that person is someone who is special to you, like a close friend, partner, or family member.

On the same token, it is important to remember that you have placed your trust in these people for a good reason and that you may not have all the facts on which to base your assumptions. Calling people out as practitioners of dark psychology can be a serious accusation and should not be taken lightly. Have a serious and heartfelt discussion with those you trust in order to understand the situation more fully and to make rational decisions about what you should and should not do to help out those you care about.

In some situations, the scenario might involve someone you do not know. There are avenues through which you can report suspicious behavior anonymously should you suspect that someone nearby is being manipulated or exploited in some way. Again, if you've got alarms going off in your brain about a potential predator, try to get past those uneasy feelings of anxiety in order to step in and check on the person whom you are worried about. You just might be the catalyst for saving someone from a lot of heartache and pain, and you may even be responsible for saving someone's life. These outcomes should be at the forefront of your mind in a situation where you feel uncomfortable. Coming off as rude or impolite is a very low price to pay compared to shrugging those feelings off and letting an innocent person walk into a potentially dangerous situation.

Conclusion

Thank you for making it to the end of *Dark Psychology 101 2021: Understanding the Techniques of Covert Manipulation, Mind Control, Influence, and Persuasion*. Let us hope it was informative and able to provide you with all the tools you need to achieve your goals, whatever they may be.

After having completed this book, you will find yourself well on your way to being a part of a population that has acted in their own interest in terms of defending against users of dark psychology. Those who seek to use these tactics against others will not always look the part, and these particular individuals are the most dangerous because they are difficult to differentiate from others with normal and benevolent intentions. For this reason, using the knowledge and educating yourself on the techniques of dark psychology is a powerful tool to use to ensure that you are not caught in a situation where you've accidentally let your guard down in response to a manipulative technique. Knowing you are a human being just like everyone else and not above being manipulated is one of the key steps toward becoming impenetrable when it comes to aggressive dark psychology techniques.

You have familiarized yourself with common scenarios and tactics used by malicious dark psychology users, and you've understood the differences between the dark triad personality types. You also have a much clearer understanding of how your body language communicates things, which you may not have been cognizant of the past before reading this book. You can use this information not only as a defense against dark psychology users but also as a way to probe and gauge whether or not the people you interact with on a daily basis are sincere or simply trying to deceive those around them.

People are not always who they appear to be, and it is important that this message is ingrained into the minds of people from all walks of life and lifestyles. No one is off-limits when it comes to dark psychology, and you are now familiar with the idea that dark psychology is being used every day on a wide scale by people who do not necessarily have bad intentions and who are not actively trying to deceive. Sometimes, emotional reactions and demeanors can influence our behaviors in ways we do not understand unless we've done the research and practiced awareness of ourselves and our actions on a daily basis. Do a favor for those you love and trust by reaching out and sharing with them the knowledge you've gleaned from this book.

Finally, if you found this book useful in any way, a review is always appreciated!

Dark Psychology Secrets 2021:

Defenses Against Covert Manipulation, Mind Control, NLP, Emotional Influence, Deception, and Brainwashing

Introduction

Congratulations on purchasing *Dark Psychology Secrets 2021*, and thank you for doing so.

The following chapters will discuss a great deal of information regarding the presence and usage of what is called "dark psychology," which refers to manipulative practices working under the radar of the victim in order to get the  practitioner something he or she wants. These goals might include any number of things, most of which are solely concerned with the benefit of the manipulator. And that is the danger of dark psychology—a practitioner who develops these skills and uses them on other people has zero concern with the ethics of the situation; they simply want something and are going to take a shortcut to get there. The cost of such endeavors involves emotional and psychic pain of a great many levels, and the damage from such experiences can last a lifetime, only somewhat assuaged by numerous types of therapy and treatment.

You may be surprised at the scope of techniques and tools which fall under the category and usage of dark psychology, and the scope of this book is to cover all of the major practices which you are likely to encounter at least once in your life. Many people have been used and abused by these practices without ever having realized it.

In chapter 1, we will discover the art of manipulation and how this works on the human mind in practice. We will discuss some of the foundational human tendencies which are exploited in common manipulation techniques and look at a few examples of these strategies in action.

Next, we will discuss how you can practice the skill of reading other people and the environment around you. In today's modern world, it has become easier and easier for people to work their dark psychology strategies while people are constantly distracted by their work, their phones, and their social lives through constant social media engagement, etc. How can you keep yourself alert and aware of when something might be amiss? We will give you some practical tips and tools for arming yourself against dark psychology schemes. As we will mention many times in this book, one of the best ways to arm yourself and prepare for any type of dark psychology encounters is to educate yourself on the different strategies involved, and this is the topic we will cover in chapter 3.

In chapter 4, we will discuss one of the most painful effects of dark psychology, which has to do with emotional manipulation. Learn how dark psychology practitioners exploit human emotion and the psychology of human behavior to get what they want at the expense of your emotional well-being. Learn to identify when this might be happening to you before we move on to a very important chapter on self-esteem.

One of the first steps a dark psychology practitioner takes is choosing a victim. This is done after a period of observation and evaluation, where they decide who is most likely to go along with their schemes. Targets who are vulnerable include those with low self-esteem and a high degree of naivete. You can guard yourself against being chosen by improving your self-esteem or, at the very least, conveying publicly that you are confident. Simple tools of body language and nonverbal communication can convey this message, even if you are still working on self-esteem and confidence. Behaviors as simple as holding your head up high with your shoulders back can influence whether a dark psychology user will move in on you or move on to someone else who seems easier to manipulate.

In chapter 6, we will discuss the practice of dark psychology in the workplace environment. Manipulation in this context happens all the time and, often, without the victims even knowing it. Learn to recognize when this is happening around you and trust your instincts when you get a bad feeling about an interaction.

Manipulative partners are our next subject and one which can be the most seriously damaging psychologically. This is because we are dealing with manipulation coming from a partner we love and trust.

In the next chapter, we will differentiate between what is an acceptable influence and what is toxic manipulation. As an easy example, think of the psychology used by a salesperson inside his store. When you walk into the store, you might expect some degree of interaction, and a sales pitch or two directed your way. The salesman might use techniques like advertising a limited-time sale or ask you questions about your life in order to use that information in his sales pitch. This is a degree of dark psychology, though it is being used in a way that is not designed to be harmful or maliciously trick another person into the desired outcome. The customer has an ultimate say and makes the decision whether or not to buy. The customer might also dismiss the sales pitch altogether before the salesman has even started, and this is her right to do so. Things like using carefully constructed arguments to persuade others to his point of view is an acceptable form of influence, while utilizing lies and inciting anger and violence in order to recruit political influence and support is an example of a toxic level of manipulation.

In chapter 9, we will discuss manipulative family members and what to do when the person manipulating you is someone you live with or have close ties to. Sometimes, it's not an option just to walk away from the situation, and you will need to have tools and strategies that you can employ in this difficult type of dark psychology situation.

Brainwashing is the topic of our next chapter. You will learn the basics and how to recognize if you or someone you know is under the influence of someone trying to employ these tactics to whatever end serves them. Though you might think you are too smart to fall under this kind of influence, many others have come forward publicly to describe how they thought the exact same way and were manipulated into belief systems and behaviors, which they never thought they could be subjected to. We are all human beings, and it is the commonalities of thought and emotion and behavior that the dark psychology user exploits.

Neuro-linguistic programming might be a term you've never heard before, but it is an important topic under the umbrella of dark psychology. Learn how behavior and thought processing can be influenced by language techniques and routine behaviors to rewire the brain.

In chapter 12, we will cover the arena of covert mind control in the form of such insidious techniques as gaslighting. In the next chapter, you will learn how to identify specific individuals in your environment who are trying to utilize dark psychology on you or others around you.

Finally, in chapter 14, we will discuss how you yourself can employ tactics of dark psychology in order to turn malicious manipulators away and to sabotage active dark psychology tactics. Learn to give such individuals a taste of their own medicine and spread this knowledge to anyone else whom you think may benefit from knowing how to stop a dark psychology user in his tracks.

There are plenty of books on this subject on the market; thanks again for choosing this one! Every effort was made to ensure it is full of as much useful information as possible. Please enjoy!

Chapter 1: The Art of Manipulation

The dictionary's definition of the word "manipulate" is "to change by artful or unfair means so as to serve one's purpose." This definition encompasses a large number of human behaviors and strategies for getting what we want, especially from other people, and the topic we will be discussing has to do with manipulation when it is done with intentional trickery that is designed to be undetected by the victim. This is what we call dark psychology.

Dark psychology is all about the human mind and changing the conditions of thought and emotion in order to get people to do things and think things they would not necessarily have of their own volition. Manipulation can be accomplished in many different ways, and it is not always accomplished consciously on the part of the user. In other words, people can behave in ways that are conducive to getting what they want from others through manipulation without having any forethought or planning to use manipulative strategies. Think of the young child who throws a tantrum or cries in an exaggerated way that is not completely genuine to get what he wants. A young child is not knowledgeable in the ways of the human mind and manipulation; she just knows through experience that her mother is likely to behave in a certain way when she cries. Manipulation is tricky in this regard, as it is used and practiced everywhere and by everyone, though the intent is not always malicious and the tactics themselves are not always readily identified. For sure, people can be manipulated by an individual who then disappears after getting what they aimed to get, never to be seen again and without the victim knowing what had happened. Often, a victim only realizes much later or after experiencing manipulation when it is too late or when the bulk of the damage has already been done. So what are some of the things that motivate people to manipulate others?

Goals and Intents of Manipulation

There are certainly too many possible answers to this question to cover all of them here, but there are some general assumptions we can make in order to pinpoint the answer to why a person chooses to use manipulation and other dark psychology techniques.

We can reasonably assume that the practitioner chooses manipulation because there doesn't seem to be another way or that it is the easiest way. Manipulation might be the last resort when other, more straightforward tactics fail. But it might also be the tactics of choice for the practitioner simply because he lacks the means or capacity to accomplish his goal by more ethically sound routes. This is the case when we talk about deviant personalities, such as the narcissism. The narcissist does not have the capacity to commiserate or empathize, or even feel compassion for other human beings. Therefore, he must put on the mask of someone who shares these traits in order to form relationships that will help him accomplish his goals. In this and other similar cases, manipulation is adopted as the preferred mode for interaction simply because the user does not or cannot interact in a more acceptable way. He knows that when his differences are detected, it works to push people away; therefore, dark psychology becomes a necessity and, ultimately, a way of life.

In other instances, a person of "normal" capacity for human relationships might turn to manipulation because it is an easier way to get what he wants. The user might recognize and even be able to feel the guilt or shame that might accompany the use of such tactics but chooses himself and his goals above the concern of others and/or his victims' well-being, emotional and otherwise. For example, a young man talking to a woman he is attracted to understands that when he lies to her in order to make her more amenable to a second date or get her to come home with him, he is doing so under false pretenses and that this may lead to emotional and psychological damage to the victim, but he decides that being able to sleep with her is more important to him than any concern about her feelings. Unfortunately, this occurs all the time and can result in either emotional or physical damage in the form of date rape or more long-term abuse and manipulation.

The goals of people who practice manipulation can be simple, complex, or nearly unfathomable to those who would never knowingly cause harm through the use of dark psychology. A practitioner may simply be looking for easy sexual encounters, or he might try to establish a long-term relationship in order to siphon emotional energy and practice control and dominance. The goal might be financially focused, or a position of power and influence, or the practitioner simply wants to earn admiration and rapport with others who are powerful and influential. The goals may be short-term, such as coming up with a distraction to a person walking by to pick something from his pocket. It can also be long-term,  such as the adoption of a complete alternate personality in order to lead a double life alongside another. The amount of planning and forethought varies quite a bit as well, depending on many different factors and intentions. Sometimes, it is impossible to understand fully why a dark psychology user operates the way he does. We will go as far as we can to understand the psychology underneath this mode of operation, but the main focus of this book is to teach you how to recognize the techniques and strategies at work and avoid becoming a victim yourself. These tools may save your life in the most extreme cases, and if you choose to share what you have learned, the life of someone close to you.

Where Is Manipulation Used?

The unfortunate truth here is that manipulation is used nearly anywhere, as long as there are people to manipulate; it's as simple as that. No person nor the environment is necessarily safe from such practice because manipulation itself is something both innate in all human beings to some degree and easily developed as a life skill for those who choose to use manipulation as part of their survival on a regular basis. Sometimes, it is used for the purpose of pleasure. We all use manipulation to some degree at some point over the course of our lives, and this occurs in any environment where we interact with other people. The difference between you and those who practice malicious dark psychology tactics is that their intents are focused and amped to the highest intensity possible to ensure that they are exercising as much influence as possible to fundamentally change the victim's mind for a period of time. The question is about the degree to which dark psychology tactics are used, and this book is all about protecting you from its most insidious and malicious forms.

Who Uses Manipulation and Dark Psychology?

Those who use dark psychology on a deep level and on a regular basis are those who are also successful in presenting to other people a persona and demeanor completely different than the one on the inside. We've all heard a story or two about a criminal who was apprehended in a community where the individual had convinced a lot of people that he was just a kind man or a regular Joe in town. These types are often the most successful, most ruthless, and who has the longest career in terms of their criminal or psychological intents against victims.

But dark psychology is not limited, as we've discussed, to the criminally oriented or those with deviant personalities. While manipulation and dark psychology can be a way of life for some, others use it for the sake of a very specific goal. For instance, take the tragic example of a young addict who uses a cycle of manipulation on his parents in order to get something he needs to feed his habit. Perhaps he disappears for weeks at a time and only comes home when he needs money to buy more drugs. He might prey on his parents' love and need to support him by playing the part of a needy son who just needs love and support to get better. Just when the parents are convinced he is on the right path, he takes what money he can from them and leaves to repeat the cycle again until he needs more support or a place to stay. This type of cycle can occur in a number of ways and manifestations. There's the jealous lover who uses control tactics to string along a partner while engaging in an affair or pursuing other interests. There's the guy addicted to gambling, who keeps asking friends and family for money while promising them he would change just to go feed his addiction and return again. Someone addicted to empathy and attention from others might make up ailments or predicaments in order to feed that emotional need and recover only to think of another ruse when she feels needy again.

Why Is Learning About Manipulation Important?

The practice and context of dark psychology and manipulation range from simple motivations to very complex long-term plans. Some readers, at this very moment, suspect they may be bending to some form of dark psychology in their lives and hope to educate themselves on how to break these cycles, while others want to safeguard themselves against the possibility of dark psychology being used on them after witnessing the harmful effects of such acts on a loved one.

Contrary to many peoples' opinions, protecting yourself against dark psychology and manipulation is not just a matter of being smart and more intelligent than the next guy. Victims of manipulation are not just "too dumb" to figure out what's happening to them. Anyone who experiences emotions and thinks like a human being is a potential victim, and those who have experienced such trauma from a psychologically abusive spouse or partner or an online scam should not feel like they are just hopelessly less observant than other people. There are things you can do to improve the chances that you will recognize and be able to act before these tactics are successfully used against you in the future. One of the most important steps is something you are already doing—educating yourself on how these people work and what the tactics look like in the moments when it counts.

Remember, guarding yourself against complete strangers who might be using dark psychology on you is one thing, but it's important to remember that those you love and trust have the most power when it comes to inflicting psychological harm. The stranger who wants to use you to some end has the initial goal of creating a relationship or interaction with you where they gain your trust, but someone who is already in your life as a person you love has probably already accomplished this goal. People who are initially trustworthy, respectful, and compassionate individuals do not often switch gears and become malicious, but you must recognize that there might be key differences between the core of those whom you choose to have in your life and those who are members of your family or already part of your life in some way. The daughter whose mother is being manipulated by her stepfather may have limited influence in terms of convincing her mother that she is being used and abused, but it is worth trying to get the mother to realize, through evidence, that something is wrong with the relationship. Sometimes, however, it is up to the victims themselves to make the real change and remove themselves completely from a situation like this. You cannot always force someone into tearing away from someone with whom they have formed a strong attachment, and one of the key tactics of manipulative partners is to sever ties between the victim and his/her family and loved ones. The idea is to make the victim's whole world revolve around the dark psychology user. With this in mind, if you suspect that someone you love is under the influence of dark psychology or manipulation with malicious intent, do not let this person tear the victim away from you if possible. Remain in their lives, no matter how much the abuser has turned the victim against you. If you recognize that the behavior is way out of character, then you can decide that there is some outside influence being injected, and this is most often accomplished through lies and complex forms of emotional and dependency manipulation. The best thing you can do is remain as close as possible to the victim until he/she is ready to realize what's happening.

If you believe someone you know is in physical danger from an abuser, it is important that you notify authorities and have law enforcement or protection agencies intervene as soon as possible.

Chapter 2: The Importance of Reading People

In this chapter, we will discuss the importance of reading people from two perspectives—the point of view of the perpetrator and that of the victim.

Reading People From a Dark Psychology User's Point of View

As mentioned previously, one of the first and most important steps a practitioner of dark psychology takes is the period of observation where he is getting ready to  pick out his victim or plan his approach for a predetermined victim. The exact situation will vary based on the practitioner's purposes. For example, someone who is looking to establish a relationship with a new victim might spend a great deal of time watching and learning all he can about a pool of potential victims, while someone who intends to get on someone's good side at his place of employment will have to work with the potential victim, along with his/her personality, demeanor, and vulnerability to manipulation. One thing to keep in mind is that not all practitioners of dark psychology simply pick out who they believe are the "easy" targets. Research has shown that a large number of narcissists actually enjoy the challenge of manipulating those "hard-to-gets" because having accomplished such a task only raises their own sense of superiority.

It is difficult to predict just how a dark psychology user chooses the victim to enact his/her strategies, but the observation and preparation period is when the practitioner will collect as much information on the target as possible before making a move. Of course, this is not always the case, especially in planned interactions that will take place on a one-time-only basis. But for the long-term victim, the practitioner must prepare carefully and devise a plan of attack that is likely to succeed if executed well.

What dark psychology cannot predict is how exactly the recipient is going to respond. In order to keep moving forward with an initial approach, the dark psychology user must be able to pick up on signals that broadcast how the victim is feeling and which give clues as to what he/she is thinking. The practiced manipulator will know what to look for in terms of body language and other verbal and physical clues to gauge how well he is doing and whether or not he needs to back off and try again later or find a new victim altogether.

The approach itself is meticulously thought through, and the demeanor and personality of the victim are often taken into account during the time when the practitioner is planning it. It is essential that the practitioner approaches in a way that is nonthreatening and friendly so as not to scare off the target. Once the interaction begins, the dark psychology user's goal is to present himself in a way that seems effortless and natural, while behind the scenes, he has put a great amount of thought and practice into this persona. His goal throughout this whole initial interaction is to gain rapport and form some kind of bond or trust so that he can open the door to further steps in his scheme. He looks for positive microexpressions and other body language cues, which will tell him whether or not the victim is comfortable or anxious. Microexpressions are very brief, telling expressions of the face which are far more subtle than the expressions we usually associate with people being happy, sad, or angry. They can last only a fraction of a second, yet if someone is watching closely, he can pick up on that brief signal, which tells him a little bit more about how the subject is feeling.

Expressions of worry or discomfort will tell the practitioner that he needs to back off or use a different tactic, though it might be too late, and he may need to simply find another target and start over. These signals are numerous and vary widely based on personality and context, so let's look at an example to illustrate how a dark psychology user might read a target in order to get clues as to how he should proceed.

Annie is sitting alone in a park, reading a book. The manipulator—let's call him David—is nearby, watching and waiting to see if she has other obligations, such as meeting someone, looking after a child, etc. He waits long enough to gather that she is there by herself, simply enjoying the nice day and relaxing with a book. He decides this might be his perfect target.

He analyzes her clothes—very conservative, no makeup, with glasses. She didn't come out here with a lot of concern about dressing up or appearing effortfully attractive, though she is cute and doesn't need to try hard. He decides she isn't completely wrapped up in herself and may not be susceptible to a flirtatious approach. She will probably respond better to a very friendly, casual encounter that does not threaten to alter her day and her plan for it. However, she is also very attentive to her book, and she may be put off by someone interrupting her. Perhaps he should give the approach and, hopefully, the conversation follows a purpose and subject, say, the book she is reading. Perhaps he will tell her he is a teacher and appreciates a young person taking the time to read and enjoy a good book.

The dark psychology practitioner goes over his plan in his head and, when he feels prepared, he will make the approach.

Now, it's all about reading the reactions and behaviors of the subject. If Annie responds with a smile and friendly effect, then this gives him a signal that his approach is appropriate and that she is open to a friendly conversation. If she is short, not bothering to raise her eyes from the book, it might be a signal that she does not want to talk to anyone right now. The practitioner might move forward with his plan until he is rebuffed a second time, then back off.

In the situation where Annie seems amenable to a conversation, he sits down and begins speaking about his vocation, interest in books, etc. As he does this, he is careful to engage her and make eye contact, but not so much that he comes off creepy. He watches the subtle cues of her facial expressions. Furrowed brows might signal discomfort, while a smile that affects the skin around the eyes is genuine and signals that she is enjoying herself. The orientation of her body also tells him something. The more oriented her body is toward the speaker, the more engaged she is. If she remains upright and straight to the front or, worse, starts to turn away, it means she is anxious and uneasy about the interaction.

The practitioner will continue to act alongside these cues until he feels it is the right time to disengage, but he will do his best to "run into her again" or, if it feels right, ask specifically to meet up with her again, perhaps for a friendly cup of coffee.

Reading People From a Potential Victim's Point of View

If we take a look at Annie's point of view and see things from her angle, we can try to get a sense of what this encounter might feel like and how you yourself should handle yourself in such an encounter. The difficulty here, if the practitioner is good, is that there has yet to be any indication that this person is not who he says he is. Or is there? Here are some red flags to look out for when a stranger approaches you and tries to engage you, for whatever reason.

First of all, Annie may have noticed the presence of this man before if she had been paying attention. Remember how we discussed how David spent some looking around and observing potential targets? One of the first things you can do to protect yourself in public is to be aware of your surroundings. When Annie first gets to the park, she might look around and take note of the people who are there and what they are doing. A man alone staring at people is going to stand out and look weird next to a bunch of couples or families, playing with a dog, or kids walking around, eating ice cream. When this man approaches, she would have recognized him as someone acting oddly, so she would be careful to keep her distance and not relinquish any personal information. Also, she would probably not agree to a second meeting, especially if she paid attention to her gut feeling of unease.

Second, the man asking for your personal information may be a red flag. You should not give up personal information to strangers in an encounter like this. The man may very well be who he says he is, but you should still be careful if you decide to see him again. This very well could turn out to be a potential romantic relationship with someone who cares about the same things you do, but this kind of process takes time, and the dark psychology user is more likely to try and expedite the process through charm and clever lies. Be wary of someone who tries to expedite a friendly relationship with you right away.

Also, someone who is lying to you about his background or anything else will often shift his eyes away while he is thinking and coming up with the lie at the moment. Pay attention to his behavior, just like he is observing you, and look for signs that he is trying hard to think and fill in gaps in his story to make himself sound more believable.  Next, you can really throw a dark psychology user off guard by asking questions. Play his game against him and make him come up with good answers to personal questions and questions about his work, his pastimes, and where he lives. Nothing is off the table. If he is a genuine, honest person, this information will roll off the tongue, and you will probably get some kind of positive gut feeling that this person is not a threat. However, if you see this man fidgeting, looking away, or looking down at the ground, then it is likely he is trying hard to think of plausible answers, and you've knocked off his concentration.

In this situation, simply put up your guard, don't offer any relevant information about yourself or your life, and feel free to enact some of those signals mentioned above, which will broadcast disinterest. Make your conversation answers short in order to bring the interaction to an end, or ask directly that you be left alone as you just want to relax and read. These things will tell the dark psychology user that he is not going to get what he wants from you, and, hopefully, he will back off. If not, it's time to notify the authorities if he continues to follow you around.

Call a friend to back you up where you are so that you do not lead him home. This is a worst-case scenario, and, hopefully, this never happens to you, but it is always good to have a plan for when something like this might occur.

Chapter 3: Manipulation Techniques

Manipulation techniques is a topic that covers a very wide range of tactics and practices, but we will cover some of the most commonly used and most insidious types of manipulation techniques here so that you have a better understanding of what is out there and how these individuals might work.

Three Modes of Persuasion

Aristotle outlined three modes of persuasion, which continue to reflect how  people communicate with one another with the intention of persuading them to a similar point of view or opinion. Often, these three modes are combined in order to have the greatest effect, especially in the arena of someone giving a speech to many people at once. In order to convince as many different personalities as possible, the speaker employs arguments focused on the disciplines of logos, ethos, and pathos.

Logos is the mode of persuasion that has to do with a logical argument. The speaker centers his statements around a logical series of facts and evidence, which is designed to lead the listener to a logical conclusion in line with his own position. This is often employed in political speeches and in many other areas where a person is trying to convince others to take action for his cause, whether that is a personal cause or something which he thinks will benefit a large number of people together. The arguments must be easy to follow and make the listeners feel as if the speaker is on the same level. It would be counterproductive to speak in terms that no one understands. The listeners might have a number of different reactions to this, including a feeling of being insulted, as well as alienated from the conversation. Persuasion in this form is considered manipulation under the loose definition of manipulation because you are employing a specific strategy in order to change people's minds and attempt to get them on your side. This strategy may also employ the use of only choosing specific information that supports your side of the argument while excluding any evidence of information that refutes it. This is one of the most common ploys when it comes to political campaigns, and two sides of the political divide might tell the same story completely differently based on what they choose to include and the type of "spin" they use to give listeners or readers a certain impression of the facts.

Another mode of persuasion, according to Aristotle, is the ethos route, which attempts to tap into listeners' emotions primarily as a way of convincing them to see the speaker's point of view. These modes can be enacted in whatever form available or preferable, such as writing in a newspaper or online, but we will stick with the visual of a speaker speaking to a group of people simply because it's a stronger illustration.

A speaker who chooses to employ an ethos mode of persuasion will often tell a story about his background or some other experience, which will work to get the listeners to feel sorry for him or empathize with him in some way. Often, these experiences are tied into his current endeavor of gathering followers and convincing them that his plans are the best for accomplishing a certain goal. The speaker might do a bit of research in order to weed out what that community's struggles are in particular and then construct his speech around the emotional impact that this issue has raised in that community. By first arousing these emotions, the speaker can then turn to what he believes he can do to change it. When listeners' emotions are impacted and evoked, they are more willing to listen to potential solutions and propositions, which may or may not align with their political or established views. The focus moves to solve that specific problem. It is necessary here, also, that the people listening are firmly convinced of the speaker's honesty and genuine empathy for the people suffering or being hurt by whatever issue is being discussed. When the people feel that the speaker is not sincere, this could potentially completely derail any momentum the speaker may have had.

The final mode of persuasion offered by Aristotle is that of pathos. In the pathos mode, the focus is on the speaker or arguer himself and presenting the most perfect and admirable picture possible to the public. He will be presented as a man of great moral character, good experience, high social and political standing, and high accomplishment. The idea here is that the people will be so impressed by the individual himself that they will be convinced that whatever he is saying or fighting for is probably a good thing because he obviously knows what he's talking about. Granted, this particular mode is rarely used alone, but it is almost always utilized when other modes are in action. For example, the introduction of a speaker to the people listening before he gives a speech is a way to condition the crowd toward a particular view of the speaker getting ready to come on stage. The idea is to impress upon listeners, especially those who are not yet familiar with him, that this person is someone who deserves attention because of all these things that he has done, stands for, or represents.

Emotional Manipulation

Emotional manipulation techniques can be incredibly malicious in nature and have the potential to cause mental damage that the victim must often deal with for the rest of their lives. This is because, in the most difficult situation, the manipulator has taken the time and made an effort to develop a sense of trust and a strong relationship between himself and the victim. Alternatively, the manipulator may have fostered a somewhat healthy relationship before choosing to do something he knows would hurt his partner and himself in some way and then gradually develops a cycle of manipulation to hide what he's done through the exploitation of his partner's established love and trust. A classic example of this is the extramarital affair.

In other situations, we are talking about a short-term interaction that employs the victim's emotional capacity and vulnerability for only the amount of time required for the manipulator to acquire some kind of short-term reward. An example of this might be someone on the street looking for some extra cash who decides to tell a passerby an elaborate story of misfortune in order to guilt the person into giving over some cash or spare change. The interaction is very short-term, and once the goal is accomplished, the manipulator moves on to his next goal.

The range of emotional manipulation techniques and scenarios is vast, but we will be focusing on some of the major and most harmful situations in later chapters, which usually involve some degree of emotional manipulation. The key here is to define what we are talking about when we discuss emotional manipulation, and it is the technique that focuses on evoking very specific emotions or even cocktails of emotional responses in order to condition the victim to be more vulnerable and help the manipulator toward his ultimate goals, whether they are aware of it or not.

There are many techniques and specific tactics that fit under the umbrella term of emotional manipulation. One of these techniques is gaslighting, in which the victim is convinced, over time, to start to doubt their reality and become confused based on a manipulator's consistent and repetitive denial and subjugation of the accusations presented to him. This is most often manifested in the form of an abuser who takes harmful actions against a victim, but when asked to acknowledge the actions, often by the abused themselves, they will completely deny that they've done anything wrong and insist that the abuser is exaggerating or making stuff up. The victim in this scenario is gradually beaten and worn down emotionally, where, at first, she may have been strong and determined to get some kind of justice through an apology, but over time, she loses this strength and begins to doubt her own sanity. This can be an extremely mentally damaging scenario because it is inflicted over a long period of time, and the brain begins to form habits and whole new paradigms concerning the reality they thought they knew.

The point here is that this type of manipulation tactic would be very hard to accomplish without having first established a very strong emotional bond with the victim. The victim stays around or feels hope that they can improve their situation because they have developed some measure of love, trust, and respect, even if this abuser is not starting to take advantage of all this. The victim herself can often be in a state of denial for a long period of time, choosing to shoulder the blame for the abuse that is going on rather than accepting that the person she loves has turned into something else entirely or that she was mistaken about him in the first place. If you can imagine and place yourself in a scenario like this with someone in your own life whom you've grown to love and trust more than anyone else, you can probably start to see how someone could become emotionally vulnerable and susceptible to mind games, clinging to the hope that what she believed she has still exists.

Power Play and Dominance

Power plays and shows of dominance are often utilized in organizations where the manipulator must have the allegiance of his followers, employees, or colleagues. The arenas where this form of manipulation comes into play range from the parent-child dynamic to the dating scene at a dance club. Or, it could be in a team meeting at work with the person wanting to show his boss that he is the  most intelligent and hardworking and that he has the most leadership potential through the subjugation of the people he is working with. Power plays and shows of dominance can be utilized in the form of simple gestures and behaviors, such as the handshake where the dark psychology user's hand takes the palm-downward position. They can also be utilized as a part of grand schemes and long-term plans that work to influence and earn the respect and admiration of groups of people, one person at a time.

The oldest and most primitive techniques aligned with this tactic involves physical presence and shows of strength. Put simply, the man with the strongest muscles and most intimidating stature might get a free pass to the competition for dominance as the male "alpha" of the group. This is a longstanding instinct, which had much use in the past when it was essential for people to stick together and also follow the same rules in order to get along and survive in a society. The same drives remain today; it is just the arenas that look a bit different.

Nowadays, you might see the example of dominance in a group of young kids who hang around each other, causing trouble and who tend to gravitate to the tallest boy, the best-looking boy, or the most charismatic. When there is a female or group of females around, it might be an unspoken assumption that the alpha gets to have the first choice before the others can make a move. This individual goes to great lengths in public to show and maintain his status among them, perhaps opting to encourage a fight that he can win in order to demand respect from anyone else who might challenge him.

But the dominance tactic can also be practiced in a much more nuanced way, such as in the corporate setting where different individuals vie for power and prominence. These people usually develop shrewd social skills that utilize manipulation in order to garner respect or even intimidation from their intended subjects. We will get into this in more detail in our chapter on workplace manipulation.

Charm and Flattery/Mirroring

Another major strategy we will introduce here involves playing on people's sense of vanity and self-awareness through the use of flattery, charm, and personality mirroring.

The saying "flattery will get you anywhere" is a pretty good summation of what's  going on when a person decides to manipulate another through the use of well-timed and effective flattery. The goal is not to overwhelm the victim, who might be suspicious of the motive. The goal is to be convincing and sincere so that she believes that the manipulator is truly taken with her in some way, be it purely physical or based on intelligence. The most basic and simple form of flattery might be to compliment a woman's smile, her dress, her makeup, and things like that. This might be used as one of the initial approach statements in order to warm up a victim for what is coming next. Granted, the manipulator has to be aware of his victims and be pretty good at gauging whether he will be successful with a certain victim or not. Some people, usually the more experienced and cynical types, will immediately turn to suspicion when someone begins using flattery on them. This is probably because they've been taken advantage of before.

This is where we can impress the importance of the manipulator's first steps of observation of potential victims again. He is going to zero in on the young, naïve individual before the stern-looking hard-ass in the corner by herself. At a party or in a public setting where there is alcohol, the abuser may pick up on the presence of young women who are having a good time flirting with lots of different men. These women may be the most susceptible to manipulation and the most affected by tactics of flattery and charm in order to get into a conversation with the dark psychology user, who may then be able to move forward with his intents.

Charm is all about apparent sincerity and entertainment. A man with a good sense of humor and conversation skills will be more capable of entertaining a victim, and the longer the abuser can keep a person engaged, the more likely he is to be successful in moving toward getting what he wants. The individual with a high degree of skill in the charm and flattery categories may be able to conjure attraction to him within the victim, further conditioning her to his will.

Lastly, mirroring comes into play when a manipulator is trying to make a target feel comfortable enough to release information that might be useful to the abuser. This often occurs in situations where an individual is trying to ingratiate himself to another who is in a position of power over him. The intent behind this behavior might be to get "in" with the people who make the decisions in order to move up the ladder, or else he might be trying to protect himself from getting on this person's bad side. This type of situation is often parodied in movies where the detective or investigator needs to infiltrate a building or a hideout, and he must work to mirror the people he comes into contact with in order to avoid arousing suspicion.

Mirroring involves simply observing the target closely and mirroring back the little mannerisms and aspects of the target's personality back to him so that he feels comfortable. This is one way in which dark psychology takes into account the basic human behaviors and tendencies, which underlie the way we all interact and form impressions of one another. A lot of these mechanisms in action happen under the radar, in the subconscious. We all react more positively in situations where we are dealing with people who are similar to us compared to the people who seem different in some way.

And it is often not just the feeling of comfort that is being affected but the established prejudices or formed opinions, having been established through our families or other experiences, which are triggered when we meet someone new. For example, if we had been brought up in a family of very devout Catholics and, for the first time, we meet someone from a different country who worships a different god, we may feel much more uneasy and unsure of the interaction compared to meeting someone from our own church, for example. This is an automatic sensation in most cases and is rooted in the evolutionary imperative that "different" often means danger, and "similar" signals comfort and safety.

In our next chapter, we will dig a little bit deeper into the mechanisms and strategies that play out in situations of emotional manipulation at work.

Chapter 4: Emotional Manipulation

In this chapter, we will work from the small-scale, short-term forms and scenarios of manipulation and move up to the most insidious, long-term examples of dark psychology utilizing human emotions.

Short-Term Manipulation

As we have illustrated in the last chapter, the example of a street beggar telling an emotional story to get a few bucks from a stranger is one of the simplest forms of emotional manipulation. The abuser has a short-term goal and plays upon one of the people's most common social tendencies in order to get what he wants. And then the interaction is over. This is a tactic that can be repeated over and over with somewhat similar results, involving a lot of different people simply because the universal human emotion of guilt and the tendency of empathy between human beings are relatively constant across a population. The only requirement for success in such a situation is for the story to be believed by the targets, and that elicits the desired emotional response.

Numerous situations reflect this same type of mode of short-term manipulation for the sake of simple, short-term goals, often in the form of money. Emotional reactions can be amped up or down, perhaps through the involvement of other people being affected, like children. A person who comes to a stranger's door asking for help might mention that his children are sitting in a car without dinner might work to elicit a stronger emotional response.

Other much more malicious intents might prey upon similar emotional responses, but the consequences of success on the part of the manipulator are much more catastrophic. For example, the serial killer Ted Bundy was famous for eliciting the help of young, naïve women through a mixture of charm and conjuring feelings of pity, mixed with a sense of urgency. He did this by wearing a cast and, in the prime moment when the victim was in view, he would fumble with a pile of books or something else as if he was trying to get them in his car and was having trouble doing it by himself. The young women would notice this and go over and offer to help, seeing that this man was having trouble. It didn't hurt that Bundy was a good-looking man, and women were often immediately enamored of him when they saw them. This immediate charm mixed with pity and a willingness to help someone in need was the perfect setting for Bundy to move in on the opportunity, usually knocking the victim unconscious before loading them in the car toward their doom.

Long-Term Manipulation

When we move into the more long-term practice of emotional manipulation tactics, we start to zero in on the necessity for the abuser to establish trust and love before enacting his manipulative intents. This could happen on the scale of a one-night stand, or the manipulator could put a plan into action that will last weeks, months, or even years. His goals might be anything from sex and money to emotional support for his own troubled and needy mind. On top of the tactics of deceit as demonstrated in the short-term situation, the abuser must be able to take on a completely different personality if the intent is to lure the target into a potential relationship, romantic or otherwise. The manipulator's intent must remain hidden, so he must conjure an alternative intention which will serve as the motivating factor for the interaction and subsequent relationship. Those personality types of dark triad often become particularly skilled in this area out of necessity and a complete lack of compassion or remorse for having duped a victim and hurt them emotionally. The abusers on the spectrum of deviant personalities, who regularly employ emotionally manipulative tactics in order to get what they want from people, range in intelligence from the highly intelligent, meticulous planner to the simple-minded, anomalistically motivated abuser. Each person on this spectrum of abusers is looking for something or a group of rewards, which correspond to some need or desire. One may be purely motivated by sex, another by emotional siphoning and control, and another by the challenge of the game. Some abusers harbor feelings of hatred and frustration and wish to inflict harm on a target because the one responsible for his pain is either dead or unavailable in some way. Emotional manipulation often becomes a necessity for someone who has not developed normally, perhaps emotionally or sexually or in the arena of social skills and, therefore, cannot form healthy relationships in "normal" ways.

Those abusers who manage long-term emotional manipulation usually have some  degree of prowess in the form of social skills or a high degree of intelligence, even if the underlying capacity for empathy, compassion, and relatability are completely lacking. They know that what they have to work with personally is not going to get them where they need to be, so the compulsion to manipulate and entice another person through fabricated feelings is so strong that they practice and learn to put the time and effort into their craft so that they are essentially "experts" in their fields.

There are also those who practice manipulation without employing study or research in order to hone these skills. These skills are part of a personality that is devoid of any capacity even to recognize that their behaviors are deviant and hurtful. These are natural manipulators who find themselves having a lot of trouble operating in the world and are much more susceptible to actively turn toward criminal activity out of frustration or anger. They are the rapists, the hired killers, the employees of those criminal actions that skip the manipulation component entirely and take what they want by force. What emotional manipulation skills they acquire are taught to them through experience or a specific teacher to utilize these skills for their specific tasks, but this will not go very far (long-term) simply because of being completely unnatural and their anathema to their innate natures.

The final topic under emotional manipulation is the long-term emotional corrosion of an abuser whose mentality changes over time through some kind of long-term influence. These abusers often bring others down with them in the form of immediate family members or close friends. These are the domestic abuse cases where a couple seemed to have a perfectly normal and happy relationship until something changed in the dynamic or lifestyle, and the relationship began to degrade. Influential factors might include things like gradual addiction to alcohol, being laid off at work, other forms of shared financial difficulty, a traumatic experience that is not processed in a way that is healthy or is faced with denial, or a sudden betrayal of trust that prompts long-lasting grudges and resentment. All of these factors may contribute to the formation of a relentless emotional cycle of manipulation and abuse, where the abuser turns all of those negative feelings and begins to project them outward, either as a weapon or as a way to avoid dealing with them himself.

In a previous example, we talked about the tactic of stringing along a victim while the abuser turns to other sources of comfort or other endeavors while keeping just enough contact in place so that the victim believes he will come back and that the estrangement is just temporary. After this experiment, the abuser might realize that this tactic actually adds to the level of attachment and desperation in the victim, thereby offering him a degree of control, which is often quite intoxicating. The abuser will continue this cycle as he sees how far he can go without prompting the victim to give up on the hope and attachment she feels.

An alternative situation is that of the jealous lover who plays mind games and demeans the victim into a place where they do not feel they deserve to have interaction with any other human beings at all, thus securing an environment of control over the victim for the abuser. The abuser will degrade the victim's self-confidence and sense of self-worth until they are no more than husks of the person they used to be.

When the abuser can reach this point, he has successfully formed in his mind the ideal victim because she has completely lost the will to fight for herself or stand up for her mental well-being. Emotionally manipulative tactics become much easier, and the abuser will only lose more and more of whatever sense of guilt or conscience he might have had once, as this way of life and dominance become easier and more like routine. He might employ tactics of yelling and intimidation to maintain this sense of control; he might punish the victim for what he calls infractions whenever the victim ventures out of his established expectations for her.

This type of situation and state of emotional degradation does not happen overnight, as we've discussed. This form of long-term abuse is a situation that gains gradual traction and momentum until it seems the train cannot be stopped. It is often baffling to friends and loved ones when a marriage or relationship that once seemed healthy goes downhill this way, but it is important to remember that no one is immune to something like this happening to them. In each situation, there is a complex set of factors and events that gradually contribute to the destruction of people's emotional strength, and eventual degradation of the bond of love and trust and respect often follows. We will discuss the importance of self-esteem in the next chapter.

Chapter 5: The Importance of Self-Esteem

Emotional manipulation preys on the subject's self-esteem in a lot of situations. Especially when it comes to women, self-esteem can be influenced and manipulated through social ideal comparative tactics, as well as personal attacks based on the subject's feelings of validation and value as a woman.

The "Ideal Woman"

In modern-day culture, especially in America, women are bombarded with a nonstop influx of images and impressions that give them a superficial idea of what or how a woman should look, feel, and act like. Often, this "ideal woman" is oblivious  to the position of confidence and self-worth that comes from inside one's self rather than the validation from others—mostly men. These women are raised in a social and popular environment that encourages competition with other women for the attention of men. Social media, magazine images, and advertisements in all their forms are all complicit in the form of emotional manipulation on a broad scale. They manipulate women's minds with the goal of trading money for self-esteem builders. But in order to be convinced to make this trade, women need to be convinced that who or what they are is not good enough. But—if they just buy this magazine with new sex tips or advice for how to dress or follow this

Instagram star who will show you how to be really sexy and give you something emulate—then just maybe, with enough time and attention, you can be good enough! This is a general message perpetuated over time and has now taken over a large part of the mental space that kids and young adults spend their time mired in every single day.

But it's important to note that men are not immune to these efforts. Images and social media pages filled with information about how to get the perfect body, how to get the women to fall in love with them, or how to juggle multiple sex partners are also all over the place. Porn can shape a young mind's idea of what sex is supposed to be like and how they are supposed to act and feel and all the things that a healthy human being would have learned through personal experience and establishing his or her own identity without such superficial outside influence. However, it is nearly impossible nowadays to be engaged with the world without being inundated with such influences, and this leads to this chapter's topic on the importance of self-esteem.

Self-esteem can be targeted by advertisements, social media, and other forms of social influence in individuals as young as 9 and 10 years old. We know this because research has shown through surveys that many girls start dieting and doing things to alter their appearances and become more socially acceptable around this time in their lives. That is a staggering realization to take in. And the pressure and influence only get stronger as we grow older and are faced with new ideas rehashed to fit our paradigms as we age, adopt new careers, and face marriage, family, etc. These images follow us around for our entire lives, so how can you foster your own sense of identity and build your self-esteem? The answers will be a little different for each individual, but the importance of addressing this issue extends to creating a form of defense against those who prey on emotional vulnerability.

One of the most efficient ways you might begin this process is to limit your exposure to social media and any media to which you compare yourself, whether consciously or subconsciously. This can be damaging on a level that we do not even recognize until we are in those moments when we are deeply displeased or  even in despair about some aspect of ourselves which we perceive others might deem unappealing or not good enough in some way. It is important to build up your own sense of self and identity, or else it becomes easy for advertisers to hijack who you believe you are and what you should be. A dark psychology user will be able to pick up on someone with exceptionally low self-esteem, especially if he is skilled in his tactics. There are certain unconscious signals that we give off when our confidence is low, and we feel self-conscious. These are indicators of a person with low self-esteem. Body language such as crossed arms and legs and a lack of eye contact, bad posture, and wide eyes that dart around without a point of concentration all signal self-consciousness and nervousness. These are like sending a signal directly to the dark psychology user, which says, "I am easy prey." The trick is to manage these body language signals and adjust them even if you are not feeling particularly confident. You can mask yourself and your unease to ward off predatory types while in public. Alternatively, figure out what it is you need in public or at work functions or parties that will help boost your confidence and lessen your self-consciousness. Perhaps sticking close to a friend would help you feel secure, or talking to someone who seems to have good social skills to teach you how to mingle and talk confidently. The worst thing you could do in a public situation is to go off alone while broadcasting your insecurity. Do not do anything to make it easier for manipulators to get to you if possible.

Self-confidence and building self-esteem on the inside rather than masking insecurity is, of course, the preferable route to building a strong defense against dark psychology users. This route is not usually easy and will look different for each individual. However, we will offer some tips and suggestions for you to try and see if they don't help you along.

Build Self-Esteem Through Meditation

First of all, set aside time each day for a brief meditation. Yes, I said meditation. If you don't know anything about meditation, don't worry. There is a lot of convoluted information out there about the practice, but the core of meditation and its practice is actually quite simple. To begin, we suggest you set aside just 10 to 20 minutes a day to be alone in a quiet place. The object of this time is to pull you away from your daily distractions in order to address that place inside of you that is insecure or less confident than the person you work hard to portray to others. You must take a look inside yourself and determine the source of your insecurity in order to address it meaningfully. If you are a total beginner with meditation, practice by simply paying attention to your breath as you breathe deeply throughout the course of your time set aside for meditation. Try to center your thoughts in the present and on your breath, and when you catch your thoughts wandering, gently redirect your focus. Don't worry about clearing your thoughts like erasing a blackboard; it will be impossible to just get rid of your thinking mind, and failing will just make you more frustrated with the process.

Let your mind wander if it wants to—and it probably will for the first few sessions—but then just bring your focus back to your breath, like a reminder now and again. Once you feel comfortable with this simple concept of meditation, try to move on to a session when you pinpoint the things about yourself from which you draw strength. Focus on the strengths rather than the weaknesses, and this will be the focus of your new meditation. What can you use to build your self-confidence? Are you good at your job? Are you hood at being a spouse or partner? Are you good at a certain craft or hobby? Whatever it is, you want to re-establish for yourself that these pastimes have value and that they make you unique. They should have more weight than the frivolous preoccupations most people have with physical appearance and impressions that come from superficial values, such as money, possessions, and position at work. It's not a bad thing to be proud of these aspects of your life if you have them, but they will never fulfill the real person inside who is asking for more in life. You cannot derive happiness and confidence purely from the influence of others; it is something you must cultivate within yourself. Make sure you are following your own path, with your own goals waiting for you at the end. Reaching such goals will renew your life and self-esteem.

Take Care of Your Health and Body

Another thing that will help you build self-esteem is to take better care of your body. The idea here is not to lose weight to become attractive to other people; it is to improve your health and boost your sense of overall well-being and confidence. Do it for yourself first and foremost, not to look good for other people. You might see areas of improvement, such as the way you eat or your exercise habits. Try to find something in the exercise realm that you genuinely enjoy so that the exercise does not just feel like an obligation. Doing this will make sure that you don't give up early on, out of boredom. In addition, finding an exercise that involves being outside will do a lot for your mood overall, which is always good. If you find that you often suffer from bouts of anxiety or even depression, sunlight and fresh air are proven remedies that can help you get back on track and find yourself and your confidence again.

Build a Support System

Another route to building self-confidence and self-esteem is to keep those who build you up close and get rid of those bad influences in your life, which you know bring you down. This can be a tricky one, as sometimes bad influences come in the form of close friends or family members. To figure out if there is something that needs attention in this category, you might consider sitting down and writing out a journal entry or some kind of list, which will help you closely consider your relationships and the influence they have on your life. Who are your best friends? How do they make you feel? Do they influence you toward unhealthy habits? Who makes you feel good, and who makes you feel bad? Is your family supportive? Do you keep close contact with those who build you up? Pay attention to how you will honestly answer these questions. Some of the answers might be difficult realizations, but this could be one of the most important steps you can take toward building yourself anew as a self-sustaining and more confident person. Another thing to look for is whether or not you are actually leaning on a poor influence, whether it's about money or emotional support. When we use others as a crutch, even if they are willing to offer support, we undermine our self-confidence in a big way. Over time, we begin to accept that we can't do anything on our own, and this becomes ingrained in our psyches and manifests as insecurity. A lot of the time, we convince ourselves that we are actually more dependent on some source of support than we actually are just because it's comfortable. Keeping in mind that there is a difference between using someone as a crutch and utilizing genuinely needed support, try to find a path toward independence from whatever is holding you back. Perhaps you are holding on to an old romantic relationship with someone simply because you are afraid of being alone, or you are holding on to an old friendship that doesn't really help you as a person and is actually intoxicating as an influence toward unhealthy ways of thinking or behavior. Whatever your situation is, it is up to you to improve it in order to progress toward your goals of becoming a more confident and independent person.

Finally, once you've pinpointed your sources of self-esteem, take steps toward strengthening those relationships, which you know help build you up as a person. If you have friends who feel good to be around in a genuine, healthy way, then put some effort into making time for them each week so that you can benefit from this positive influence. Something that might help a lot is to have an open discussion with this friend or group of friends about what you are trying to do in your life and how you want to work toward building self-esteem. These people are probably the ones who know you better than anyone else, so they may have some valuable input for you in terms of who they perceive you to be and what they feel are areas where you seem to struggle and which you may not have noticed before. These positive relationships may be family instead of friends, or perhaps even your own partner whom you haven't had a lot of time for recently. When we make time to have genuine face-to-face interactions with the people who hold value in our lives, we get a lot more out of the experience than if we are constantly distracting ourselves alone or in groups with media and other things that keep the personal interactions from happening. This often turns into a safe place that chases away the anxiety of having to open up to other people, but it will lead to nowhere but isolation, loneliness, and emptiness. Truly positive relationships that help you build yourself up as a person are built on the foundation of being a safe, open, and honest place to talk about the things that are not so comfortable or happy or superficial. People need to be able to talk about their problems and insecurities, so do your best to get past that initial anxiety about upsetting the tranquil, superficial waters, and take a risk with the ones you truly trust, love, and respect. When this happens, you are likely to find that your friends, who are positive influences to you, or group of loved ones have the same craving as you and will appreciate the opportunity to open up a new outlet for interaction and relationship. Spend some time listening to the concerns and problems of your friends as well. Encourage a relationship where there's free communication in a way that is nonjudgmental. We are struggling with something, so be as supportive to your friends as they have been for you. Relationships built on trust will be a huge asset as you change certain things about your life in order to build self-confidence and self-esteem.

Chapter 6: Workplace Manipulation

Workplace manipulation takes many forms, so we will look at some examples from different people's points of view.

Using Manipulation to Climb the Corporate Ladder

Most often, workplace manipulation is about building one's own prestige within  the environment for the sake of pursuing self-centered goals. But there are lots of different nuanced forms of manipulation that take place in the office and other workplace environments, which are not necessarily consciously undertaken. A lot of the time, it boils down to people's sense of importance when it comes to how others view them and what their positions are within the company. Let's illustrate something like this that might be going on inside the boardroom meeting of higherups within a company.

We'll say that this company is pretty sizeable and competitive within its industry, with lots of people working on the upper management side as the company expands and works to manage its locations. Each individual here holds some level of power over certain areas and branches of the company, but there is room for people to move up as the business continues to do well and positions open up in order to manage more and more property. You can bet that this upward mobility currently present within the company is one of the primary thoughts on these people's minds as they interact with their bosses and conceive ideas for growth in an effort to impress those who are in charge and those who make company-wide decisions. This is an area where politics may come into play and where manipulation tactics related to politics are working from both sides. A top executive might push himself forward by offering ideas and refuting the ideas of others in order to make himself look like the smartest one in the room. Such actions might prompt other people in the room to form alliances against him in order to tear him down or to make room for themselves.

Using Manipulation to Defend One's Position

On the flip side, those in the top positions will feel a need and desire to hold onto power through demonstrations of dominance and domineering tactics even when they are not entirely applicable or necessary in order to prove the point of his/her seniority and position. Now, of course, this doesn't apply to every person in a place of power within a company, but there is certainly an argument to be made that those instincts which prompt people to exert themselves in order to maintain control of a population would be triggered in a position of power. At these positions, the stakes become higher and blame is often placed on those at the top of a company. Therefore, actions of manipulation might stem from fear, which is a very strong motivator toward actions and decisions that may not be entirely ethical but rather a desperate attempt to hang on to power and influence and make sure no one crosses him/her in his/her decisions. People who make it to the top of a prestigious company often let this kind of position and power go to their heads in different ways, manifesting as a domineering presence that must be obeyed and bowed to for fear of being cut out of the game entirely. This kind of dominating presence is often fueled by a growing desire linked with greed and power-hungry cravings, which only manifest once the individual has had a taste of the power that seems to win them such prizes. There is a whole area of research surrounding the phenomenon and effects of power on the individual psyche, but corruption is a common consequence.

We've seen this unfold all over the news in America where people at the highest echelons of power seem to hit a point somewhere along the line where they no longer make business decisions that involve the interests of the people responsible for holding the company up, but which seem solely concerned with the unstoppable growth and dominance of the company within its industry. This is, after all, one of the most important aspects of working and managing a company that is ingrained in employees from the moment they start working. The capitalist economy is all about growth and economic dominance. The leaders consider themselves ultimately responsible for this aspect of the business and often make decisions that minimize the importance of those at the bottom while doing whatever it takes to increase the profits coming in. The mode of control for individuals in these positions is often to practice manipulation techniques.

In order to make sure everyone within the company is doing their jobs and keeping nothing in their minds except perfect operation, the people in power must persuade and charm their underlings so as to convince them that their work is thoroughly appreciated and vital to the successful operation of the company. This is done through lots of attention to the business statement of purpose and how the company improves society and offers something of value to everyone involved and to all customers helping to keep the company going. These value statements often seem completely altruistic in nature, as if the ultimate aim of the company is to help this specific niche of human individuals, and this goal goes far beyond simple monetary concerns as the primary objective. In this way, workers can be inspired to do their jobs to the best of their ability with the belief system that they are working for the people who are buying their products, and not just to boost the income of the people who are in charge and running the company from the top. This is a form of internal and nonpersonal manipulation, with decisions and actions being taken from the top, which then spread throughout the company through different modes of communication and dissemination of information through such individuals as middle management in order to get to those on the lowest "rung" of the corporate ladder. As this is done, it soon becomes part of the paradigm of working there, and it becomes an essential part of the public identity of that company.

This all seems sinister on the face of it, but it is all about the balance that is demanded from a market economy between filling a need within society and also building up the business so that it becomes dominant in the industry and remains successful and sustainable. There is nothing wrong with maintaining a proper balance between these two concerns, but, all too often, the scales start to tip toward economic dominance within an industry and the greed of those in power. This movement prompts manipulation as a necessity to maintain the façade of the balance, which may or may not have existed at the outset.

Now, let's scale down a bit and talk about how an individual employee might utilize tactics of manipulation in order to build himself up above everyone else. There is a tendency within groups of human beings that is quite effective in this context. For example, a boss assigns a group of employees to work as a team on a certain project. They are to meet and  brainstorm ideas to come up with a detailed plan on how to proceed. An employee who has his sights set on climbing up the ladder can use this situation to his advantage if he plays it right.

The person in group meetings who talks the loudest and is the most charismatic will have an instinctively more profound effect on the minds of those around him compared to the one who sits back in the corner or talks in a quieter tone of voice and affect. Even if this quieter individual has the better ideas, the group will tend to lean toward the one with much more confidence, and this is something that is ingrained within us as human beings, in relation to the establishment of an alpha or leader, which goes back to the first manifestations of human society on earth. We can't get away from the tendencies tied to human nature, though we can work to be conscious of when someone is using this as a part of manipulative tactics. Without thinking about it, however, the team will automatically start to lean toward this confident, charismatic voice in the room, and, ultimately, this individual will use this phenomenon as a way to make himself seem like the prominent voice of leadership from the perspective of his boss—and this is the ultimate goal.

Unfortunately, because of this phenomenon, many bad decisions are often made without the realization that they were not the best ideas until it is too late. The fact that this is an often subconscious mechanism of human nature means it is not always something that people realize is happening to them at the moment when they are making those crucial decisions.

Using Manipulation to Gain Power Over Colleagues

Another manipulation tactic that people often see in the workplace is that which works to belittle and undermine others as a means to make themselves feel better or superior in their positions. The irony is that, often, people who enact this kind of insidious manipulation in the workplace do not hold positions of power above those they demean. This can actually be one of the primary drivers for someone to behave this way against other people. Especially men who feel that they are not in the position that is commensurate with what they feel they deserve will be susceptible to the temptation to act out their frustration and take it out on others with whom they interact on a daily basis. This is simply convenient for them because of the ease of access and their availability to become easy prey. The manipulator in this context will quickly learn who in their environment would make good targets. In other words, these are people who are unlikely to fight back or defend themselves. Here, we return to the concepts we've discussed in previous chapters about how the manipulator will choose his prey. Will he go after the diminutive and weak-willed, self-conscious young woman who has just started at the company or the confident woman who doesn't take crap from anyone? The answer should be obvious. Therefore, it is essential that those in the environment look out for one another when it comes to defending against manipulation in the workplace.

Unfortunately, people do not always take it upon themselves to look out for one another in an increasingly individualistic society that operates on an everyone-for-himself basis. In addition, the manipulator may be smart enough to know that he must operate in a way that is not obvious to the other coworkers around him. He will pinpoint and target a single individual and take opportunities when he can, perhaps even convincing the target to take on extra workloads. The effect here would be that the manipulator feels a sense of power that is false but nevertheless comforting. The manipulative tactics utilized in this context are most often that of belittling and undermining the already low-confidence level of the target. The target will start to feel as if she has no choice as she is persistently told that she needs to get better at her job and take on more responsibility in order to be noticed. Alternatively, the manipulator might employ tactics that focus on engaging the target's good-natured feelings and tendencies. These would include feeling sorry for him and like she should help him, that he is genuinely in need of support and assistance, and that she should feel guilty for not wanting to help him. These feelings can be evoked through direct confrontation with the manipulator as he drops subtle cues to trigger these emotions. The effect may not take place right away, but most of the most malicious dark psychology tactics begin with the planting of simple, unnoticed seeds of doubt and emotional manipulation, which grow over time.

In this way, workplace manipulation can work just as effectively as manipulation situations at home because a person often spends almost as much time at the office working as they do at home relaxing. The psychic effects of workplace manipulation can be just as harmful and can make the target feel trapped. Not everyone feels they have the capability to just pick up and leave a job, especially if they have become invested in their careers. People put up with unpleasant interactions at work every day for the sake of responsibility for the wellbeing of their families. Unhappiness and dissatisfaction in the workplace can lead to others viewing you as a way to alleviate their own stress through covert abuse and emotional manipulation. On the flip side, those who feel as if they are under a large amount of stress may become the perpetrators of such workplace abuse as a way to alleviate their stress and not even realize they are turning into this kind of person. We all do what we can, sometimes unconsciously, to alleviate stress from whatever source. These mechanisms can happen automatically and without conscious thought—just like when something happens, and we get suddenly very frustrated and angry. We seem unable to control the feelings that arise and, if we are not careful, may form habits of reaction in these situations which are harmful, either to ourselves or those around us. It is important that people do not underestimate the psychological effects of their stress and their reactions to that stress on other people, most often on the people they love the most.

Sometimes, all it takes is for someone to point out to the abuser that his behavior is out of line. He may not realize the extent to which he has let his automatic reactions to stress get out of hand. If this tactic does not work, then it may be necessary to notify a manager or supervisor in order to have the behavior addressed. If you find yourself the target of workplace manipulation and abuse and cannot successfully address it yourself, then you need to seek out help and support in order to make the behavior stop. Perhaps you can move departments or surround yourself with a different team. Your boss or supervisor should take this kind of thing seriously and take steps to alleviate the effects of such abuse and put a stop to the abuse itself. Do not underestimate the long-term effects of just taking it upon yourself to put up with it and deal with it. A lot of people start out thinking they are too strong to be affected by long-term abuse, but the human psyche only has so much it can put up with before it starts to give in. Enlist the help of those you trust to help you navigate the situation.

Chapter 7: Manipulative Partners

One of the most malicious and harmful forms of manipulation happens in the place that most of us believe is the most comfortable and safest to spend our time—inside your own home.

But the truth is, people live out years and even decades of their lives under the  influence of a manipulative partner. We read stories and headlines all the time about the manipulation that can happen inside the home and how sometimes it can lead to physical altercations, abuse, and even spousal homicide. The manipulation that occurs inside the home between partners employ the most powerful and influential forms of emotional manipulation in existence, and it works on a scale that tampers with the very souls and hearts of the targets.

When a form of manipulation by a partner is very successful, it is because the manipulator has been able to pinpoint exactly where the partner is most vulnerable emotionally. This area of vulnerability will be different in each person, and, certainly, there are those who are much more manipulatable than others of a stronger constitution and higher emotional intelligence. We will focus on some of the most common emotional strategies employed by manipulators in the home.

Flattery and Superficial Charm

Superficial relationships employ superficial pleasures and techniques. These are the kinds of relationships that might start through an initial sexual encounter and sustain themeselves based purely on the initial excitement and pleasure coming from an exciting new affair, extramarital or otherwise. Predators in this arena often juggle multiple partners at the same time and become quite talented at compartmentalizing each interaction and keeping them separate from each other. This is vital to a successful manipulative tactic in this context because he, most often, will employ excessive charm and flattery in order to put the target in a place psychologically where she is most susceptible. As with all of the most skilled dark psychology users, the practitioner will have picked out his target specific to his intentions and tactics. Those women who spend all of their time on their looks and making themselves public on social media are often the most susceptible to flattery and superficial charm tactics. They enjoy the attention and compliments, and they often form a kind of addiction to this attention, using it as a way to sustain themselves and their self-esteem. When they don't get this attention, their esteem and confidence might plummet to a place where they become desperate, often utilizing sexual influence in order to garner the attention and admiration they've developed such a need for.

This type of tactic can be quite economical for the manipulator because talk is cheap. When a person's self-esteem and trust stem simply from a steady influx of flattery and charm, that person can be pretty easy to string along for a decent amount of time. If there is financial support coming in as well, then the target can be quite satisfied to turn a blind eye to behaviors that might be the antithesis to the things she is hearing from her partner.

Superficial means of control and manipulation are effective for short-term gain, but the effects of this behavior often catch up to the manipulator in some way or another. The targets of such manipulation are also susceptible to being stolen away, as the emotional attachment present in deeper types of emotional manipulation does not take hold in the same way regarding this superficial charm- based manipulation. Anyone who comes along with more material wealth and steady use of charm and flattery may ignite a desire to switch gears, stemming from a mentality that the "grass may be greener on the other side." Without the bond of love or trust holding her back, this might be an easy choice to take. When this situation arises, it is common for the manipulator to act out in the way of violent or abusive behavior in order to keep his targets "in line." Jealousy and the need for control and dominance often accompany the desire to gather "trophies" through superficial manipulation, and the prize of maintaining control over his prey is not grounded in a deep, fulfilling relationship, but rather the status that comes along with "owning" a woman.

Women are just as capable of stringing along a man, perhaps through a much more powerful persuasion tactic of sex and desire. Those men who are obviously drawn to and dominated by the pursuit of women are easy targets for predatory women of this type. It is easy to pick out these types of men in a crowd or to simply attract them through flirtation. Men can be susceptible to letting down their guards emotionally when they choose to prioritize sex in a relationship. In order to support these desires and fool themselves into thinking they are being fulfilled on a deeper level, they can buy in all sorts of psychological manipulation techniques, which work to convince the target that there are real love and respect within the relationship. Women who are skilled in this type of manipulation will be quite insidious in their mixture of tactics, turning the tables and inciting guilt  when they see the opportunity to make their target feel bad for something they did. They can ignite their partner's sense of protecting what's theirs and even encourage the partner to act unethically on the predator's behalf, all in the name of a false claim of love.

Gradual Emotional Breakdown

This form of psychological manipulation and abuse adheres to a principle of kicking the target while she's down. Over time, the target is told over and over again that she is not good enough in some way. Once the manipulator figures out what is most painful to the victim, he may use this as his weapon in this regard. For example, if the target feels self-conscious about her physical appearance, this becomes the abuser's subject of torture, and he will use the weapon often, especially if he sees it effectively breaking down the mental strength and composure of the victim. Doing this offers an unchallenged level of control and influence over the victim, and, once there, the abuser will continue to exercise the tactic in order to keep her in that low place. This kind of emotional abuse is often accompanied by physical abuse, as well. The target who has been worn down through emotional abuse will also be unable to defend herself effectively, as the will to live itself is broken down alongside any sense of self-confidence or identity. The reward for this type of abuse works differently for the abuser in a lot of these cases. He is not usually trying to gain something from the victim but is rather releasing the frustration, anger, or depression that he feels himself and is unable to deal with. He passes along this pain in order to alleviate himself of some of the stress and pressure in some way, often functioning in complete denial of his actions as a way to live with himself as he continues this behavior.

Most of the time, there is no winner in these unfortunate circumstances. Both parties are spiraling downward. The longer this behavior continues, the more obscure the way out becomes. Other factors complicate this situation, such as kids and financial status. Women may feel trapped within an abusive relationship because they depend on the partner for financial support or other kinds of support. There might also be the threat of physical harm to the children should the victim take any action toward getting out of the situation, to get either her children or herself away. At this point, the abuser is driven by the simple and basic drive to possess and control without any concern as to what he is actually gaining out of the situation. This feeling will often persist in situations where the abuser has lost control in all other aspects of his life or in situations where he was brought up in a similar environment and understands no alternative way to live and operate in relation to other people.

Attachment and the Fear of Loss

Another type of manipulation in romantic relationships is one that preys on a person's fear of loss and sense of attachment or addiction to the manipulator. This can be one of the most effective when it comes to long-term manipulation because of the strength of the target's fear and aversion to loss or doing anything to jeopardize losing possession. Many people don't think of themselves as being addicted to possessions, but the truth is that when a person develops a relationship with another human being, part of that presence is a formed attachment that receives reinforcement the longer he/she stays with that partner. Love can be gained and lost over time, but the attachment and habitual presence of a partner can be something that is very hard to overcome, and this is what makes the loss of a loved one or partner so difficult to manage, even if there has been an estrangement in terms of romantic love or affection.

The manipulator who chooses this path is often much more intellectually involved with the process than someone who chooses a different, more emotionally, and superficially based tactics, such as the situations discussed above. This kind of manipulation takes a bit of forethought and planning, as well as a good sense of timing and the ability to read a potential target and victim.

A lot of success in this particular tactic depends on the nature and personality of the victim. That is why choosing a victim who is susceptible to being controlled and manipulated in this way is an important first step should the manipulator have the opportunity to choose. Alternatively, this type of manipulation might manifest later on as changes take place in the relationship and the more dominant partner decides to take advantage of this trait in order to maintain control or gain access to some different type of reward. Once this vulnerability is known to the abuser, it is just a matter of time before he can enact control over

the target using threats such as abruptly leaving the victim and arousing the fear of abandonment. The abuser may threaten to divorce the subject or leave him/her for another partner, or the abuser may play around with these kinds of threats by talking about how desirable another person is, how he/she might like to be with that person if they weren't with the target and other situations of that kind. Doing this over and over will cause the target to doubt more and more her own capability of staying in a relationship and "keeping" a man at her side. This will build toward the degradation of self-confidence and identity, playing into a whole new level of emotional manipulation as described in the previous sections.

The tactic of pulling away, stringing along behind, then rewarding with a brief return is one way to put this tactic into hyperdrive. That period of alone time without the partner can often work to inflame that sense of fear and anxiety about the loss so that when the partner does finally throw the target a bone, she responds with desperation and a willingness to go along with anything the partner wants in order to get him back into her life.

All three of these manipulation tactics used within relationships can be effective alone or together as a combination of tactics. The decision regarding the tactic being used is often dictated by how much the target begins to show her colors regarding her own emotional vulnerabilities. The abuser who chooses to pay attention to these signals and then exploits those areas of vulnerability is a malicious type of an abuser who has chosen to put his own emotional needs and desires ahead of that of the partner or target he has chosen. Sometimes, this switch to an abusive spouse happens down the road, following a traumatic event, and sometimes, this is something the abuser will go to great lengths to hide until he is married and feels secure in his position of power and dominance over the partner. Other times, the manipulator has been an abuser his whole life, being in possession of one of the dark triad personality types. He has become an expert in this particular field and has possibly put a lot of thought and preparation into his choice of partner and how he will enact his manipulation tactics and control after the relationship has been established under false pretenses.

Just as a mother of a son who becomes a violent criminal cannot often completely lose the love and attachment for her child, the partner of an abusive partner may find it incredibly difficult to tear herself away from the situation when she has grown to truly love the abuser and has formed a strong bond and sense of attachment to him. As mentioned before, the additional factors involved, such as children, can work against the victim to keep her locked in a situation. This makes her feel trapped and as though she cannot go to anyone else for help, whether she's been threatened directly by the abuser or these fears are only in her head.

Chapter 8: Acceptable Influence vs. Toxic Manipulation

We've covered quite a bit of ground regarding the manifestations of dark psychology in society and how some of these tactics are considered to be among the malicious and psychologically damaging forms of abuse in existence. However, it is important to remember, as specified in our first chapters, that the use of dark psychology is spread over a wide spectrum of behaviors and intentions, not all of which are insidious and with the intention of inflicting harm or exploiting other people's vulnerabilities to an unethical level. The point at which this line can be drawn might differ from person to person, but in this chapter, we will discuss how to discern between an abusive manipulator and someone who is employing a low level of manipulation with much less malicious intentions.

There is no perfect formula for deciphering what a person's intentions are or whether he is knowingly employing tactics of dark psychology. It is up to you to make decisions regarding how you will proceed with interaction when something feels amiss, and it is important that you follow your gut instincts when it comes to these types of feelings. Often, the subconscious mind knows things that it cannot communicate directly to the conscious mind. So, if you feel red flags are going up, and your nerves are standing on end, even if you're not sure why it is probably a good idea to remove yourself from the interaction or take steps to make sure things do not progress.

Tolerable Manipulation and Influence

Low-level manipulation tactics are those strategies that are involved in things like sales pitches and political speeches. These forms of persuasion are employed using certain information about the human psyche but are not intended to directly hurt the person or explicitly misguide them. Even in the realm of politics, where the lines between ethical use and unethical use of persuasion tactics can be blurry, the facts can be sorted from the nonfacts, and people are left to their own devices when it comes to the ultimate decision of whether to vote for a particular individual or not. However, the use of such tactics like disseminating hateful ads or intentionally divisive ads throughout social media is one tactic that has come under fire in recent days. Though you are not directly forcing a person to make a personal decision with these tactics, you are substantially altering the psychological environment that will ultimately make the decision under the stress of having been influenced in a visually staggering way. Again, the line here can be blurry, as typical political ads often try to trigger those emotional responses that we talked about during our discussion o the three modes of persuasion. Additionally, everyone is probably going to have a different opinion about where that line actually is. Should we not allow social media to throw targeted ads at us based on our data? Should we report someone in a store who is trying to get us to feel bad about not donating to such and such cause?

The best we can do as individuals is to safeguard ourselves by being in control of the type of situations we put ourselves into and being always aware of the possibilities. Just like in our example with a salesman in a store, when a customer voluntarily walks in there, she knows that, at some point, she is probably going to be approached by someone trying to sell her something. She walks into the store even though she knows this and makes the decision that she is willing to tolerate this interaction for the sake of picking up whatever she needs. When you listen to a news show or a pair of talking heads in a debate, you know that each of them is going to try to throw arguments and facts at you in an effort to convince you of their way of seeing things, but it is up to you to actually research and make sure that what these people are saying is accurate and to make judgments and decisions for yourself. Protecting yourself means being aware of the possibilities while not outright turning yourself into a totally cynical person who never trusts anyone in any capacity. There may be an honest, young gentleman who crosses your path today needing help with a flat tire. The decision is yours as to what you will do following this event. Do you let down your guard a little to help the man? Or do you refuse based on the fear of the unknown? Well, the answers are different for each of us. It is for us to take into account the circumstances surrounding the situation.

Play the role of the detective in order to help you discern whether a situation is reasonably safe or if there is some risk involved. Look for the signs that someone is not completely honest with you during an interaction. We've discussed some of the things you may want to watch out for during an interaction with a stranger, which may give you some clues as to whether the person is genuine or not. In addition to this, remember to take a step back and be aware of your environment at all times. Are you in a place where it might be easy for someone to catch you off guard? Next time you have to go somewhere for whatever reason at night, consider taking along a friend to ensure safety in numbers. Never offer your trust willingly when you are in a situation that feels unsafe or not completely comfortable. Listen to your gut in situations like these where it could be up in the air as to what a stranger's intentions are for talking to you.

This mindfulness about your surroundings and the circumstances of interaction should extend to online interactions as well. Never give out personal information to someone you've never met in person. Do not trust that everyone you talk to online is exactly who they say they are. A lot of people make use of dating sites and have successfully found partners online, which is a wonderful thing. However, it might be wise to stick to those most reputable sites if you decide you want to try this route for whatever reason. Signing and participating in a site that charges a monthly fee or another kind of financial commitment helps them weed out and avoid those people who are just trying to get in somewhere to meet someone and manipulate them off the cuff. Those who take their time with a profile and are willing to pay a fee for the services offered on the dating site are more likely to be genuinely invested in the endeavor.

Also, never agree to meet someone in person for the first time at a private residence or otherwise non-public place. Always assume the worst when it comes to such interactions until you have had a chance to see otherwise. Make sure that you are meeting at public places, and consider taking along a friend if you are feeling especially nervous about meeting someone for the first time. As an additional test, make sure to pay attention to the information exchanged online, though it shouldn't be personal information at this stage. Remember the likes and dislikes and the more mundane things included in the profile so that you can quiz the individual in subtle ways when you meet in person. If the person you are meeting seems to be familiar with the subject matter and recognizes immediately when you mention something from their profile, this is a good sign that they are being real with you. If you mention these things, but the person seems to struggle to maintain composure and make things up to fill in the gaps, then this could be a red flag that the information shared on his profile is not genuine and simply rehashed from another profile or made up entirely. You can never be too careful in this arena, so do what you can to stay aware. Make sure you can trust the person through in-person interaction.

Not All Intentions Are Malicious

With all of these said, it is also important to remember that people sometimes utilize subtle and minor forms of manipulation, which are not malicious in nature, as a way to present the best of themselves to someone new. It is something that is pretty universal across the young dating world. People going on their first dates are always pretty mindful of themselves and the person they are presenting, either because they are afraid to show their true selves just yet, or they want to make sure they don't do something silly out of nervousness. Different personalities deal with this kind of anxiety in different ways, so don't completely  discount a person for fumbling over a few words or talking about something that is not openly discussed on their profile in the case of an online to in-person interaction. It is best not to live in complete fear of every single person you meet in person and online as if they are a potential threat to your physical and mental well-being. While this book is all about manipulation and protecting yourself from it, it is also very important to realize that living life itself is always going to involve risk, and sometimes, it is necessary to accept risks for the sake of what you might gain or the fact that you gain fulfillment and satisfaction on a very personal level from whatever activity or endeavor you are thinking of embarking on. There is no way to safeguard yourself against danger in every aspect of your life completely. If you tried to do this, you would probably end up locking yourself in a room and never venturing to experience anything else in your life. This is no way to live, so try to maintain a mental balance between being careful in your day-to-day interactions and activities while also being brave enough to live your life.

Chapter 9: Manipulative Family Members

Perhaps right alongside manipulation between romantic partners is manipulation that is exercised between family members, and this is one of the most hurtful and toxic experiences a person can go through. In this chapter, we will go over some example situations in which dark psychology can operate between family members in a home or close family members living apart. The first dynamic we will discuss is that between a parent and child.

The Child as the Manipulator

When you were young, do you remember your parents using certain tactics on you as a way to show you that something you did was wrong or to punish you? Some of us talk about the guilt factor involved when a parent would simply look really hurt and explain that she is disappointed as a way to make the child feel bad for his actions. This took the place of physical punishment, and I think a lot of us would say that this form of emotional punishment utilizing guilt and shame can be worse than a spanking.

As a child grows older, she may employ manipulation tactics in order to deceive or mislead parents so that they can do things that are normally not allowed. This is considered pretty typical behavior for teenagers to most people, though it can be infuriating and frustrating for parents trying to guide and protect their kids.

When manipulative tactics turn toxic and cause long-term harm, a vicious cycle of hurt and mistrust can form where there was once love and trust. Abusing another's love for you for the sake of getting something from them is a hurtful and damaging path. Let's look at an example to see how this might unfold.

A couple of attentive and nurturing parents raise a son named Derek. Derek is a well-behaved kid all throughout grade school and middle school, but in high school, he starts getting involved with kids who are always drinking and partying. They also introduced him to drugs. At first, he just partakes every once in a while when he is at a party, but after his first two years in high school, he realizes he has developed a kind of dependency on it and craves the drugs several times a week. He has someone to buy from in connection with his friends at school, but he doesn't always have the money. To get cash, he asks his parents and makes up an excuse for needing money. He has not been getting in trouble with the school, and his parents do not know about his behavior outside of school. They miss him more and more because he seems to be gone so much, but he does not really open up to them often.

In this situation, a kind of trade-off turns into a vicious cycle, and Derek picks up on how he can manipulate his parents to get what he wants because he knows what they need from him. When he needs cash, he also takes a night to spend time with them and talk to them about school and basically just tell them what they want to hear—that he is doing well and he is happy and healthy. At the end of the conversation, once he feels he has made some key connections with them, he says that he needs money for something reasonable. Maybe he says he just met a girl and wants to take her out, or he needs money to help with a project or event at school because he is part of a committee or something like that. His parents, now warmed up because they have gotten to spend a little time with him,  agree to give him some cash and are even a bit generous. After this happens, he disappears for the next two nights, perhaps texting his parents to let them know he will not be able to make it to dinner but sometimes forgetting. The cycle continues all the way through high school, and after high school, he genuinely tries to get a job but finds that his drug use puts him in a state where he can't really function as he needs to in order to keep a job, and the addiction has just grown stronger.

His parents, in this situation, are the most tragic component here in a lot of ways emotionally. They have raised a son whom they love more than anything, yet he is pulling away. They begin to suspect that he is not as healthy and happy as he was when he tried to convince them in high school. Perhaps they finally pick up on the possibility that he is doing drugs and not doing well academically around his third or fourth years of high school, so they try to talk to him, but he denies everything. He keeps asking for money and occasionally coming home and spending time with them at dinner and having conversations afterward, but he doesn't open up much about his social life, and he always asks for money at the end of it. When they are hesitant, and they ask him about where the money is going, he gets defensive, accusing them of not loving him anymore. Or he breaks down crying and trying to evoke feelings of pity and guilt so that they might relent. The parents may realize, at some point, that they are being played, but they are so torn because of their love and concern for Derek.

Unfortunately, this is not such an uncommon situation nowadays. Kids are getting out of school and finding it difficult to get a good job or being inundated with influences who are into drugs and criminal activity to make money instead of working. Loving parents find themselves in a place where they wonder what went wrong, and they despair about the state of their kids, yet they are tethered unconditionally by their love and can never say no when their child comes home and asks for support because they are so desperate to spend time with him and try to break through that shell he has put up around himself. They are desperate, just as much as Derek is to get what he needs to feed his habit.

Cycles like this one can last for years and years as the parents continually try to reach the son, while the son continually comes home, begging for cash or a place to stay for a night or two. One constant thing in this cycle, which keeps feeding it, is the promise that things are going to change or that he is going to get help and be better and that he just needs some cash to help him get started. The lies and emotional manipulation continues while the parents are strung along behind, desperately hoping for a miracle and unable to shut their son out or refuse him help.

Situations like this one do not often have easy endings, though sometimes, the child successfully completes rehab and then struggles with everything he has to  change and kick his habit for good. People do this through all kinds of different support networks, sometimes religious affiliations or charity organizations where they completely reorient their focus and surround themselves with support to help them stay away from the temptations of their old lives. The cycle can be broken, but it is a hard road where emotions are involved in manipulation techniques over time.

The Parent as the Manipulator

Now, we will look at an example of emotional manipulation where the tables are turned—the child is the victim of abuse by the parent.

A young girl named Anna has grown up with her mother and a stepfather who has never really concerned himself with developing a relationship with her. The two met when Anna was 11, and now, she is 13 and getting ready for high school. Anna's mom spends as much time with her as possible, though Anna's stepfather often forms a divide between them as he introduces ultimatums about who Anna's mom will spend time with and how he will leave if she can't pay enough attention to him. In this situation, both the mother and daughter are under the influence of emotional abuse, but in different ways. The mother feels that she has a responsibility to both, though the husband tries to manipulate her into feeling as if she is neglecting their relationship. The daughter is made to feel as if she is taking time away from her mother and stepfather, and she sees the clearly visible frustration and the rage that develops whenever she comes to her mother. This happens especially when she seeks attention and support as she enters high school and is nervous about changes.

The way the stepfather maintains this kind of emotional abuse cycle is when the victim relents and gives him what he wants—mostly an admission that he is right and they are wrong and an apology. He then responds with apparent warmth and understanding and gives them just enough hope that he might be changing to keep the relationship going. The daughter is not at the point where she is going to lash out and try to yell some sense into her mother, and the mother does not yet feel that her husband's requests are inconsiderate or selfish. This is all because of the way he responds when they finally relent to his wishes. He says things like, "I'm sorry for the way I acted" or "I know I am being selfish; I just really care about you," etc. He learns over time what is effective and what is ineffective and pays attention to the reactions he gets when he uses different strategies to evoke emotional dependence and sympathy. It is an insidious thing to do in a relationship, especially when the victims are susceptible to compassion and empathy and are naïve. Both victims want to believe that they are not in a dangerous or toxic situation, and they grasp onto the kernel of hope each time a bad interaction ends. This acts as the fuel that moves the situation forward as it escalates, all the while making the victims believe they are making headway and coming to an understanding.

This situation is a prime hunting ground for the manipulator, who may start to use different manipulative tactics to enforce control and dominance. The stepfather may be driven by a number of different motivators that are mostly unfathomable to people who are not in that position. He may be jealous of the two young women's bond and acts out of frustration with this, trying to drive them apart and force himself between them. There may outside factors involved, as we've discussed, which lead him to act out on the only people he feels he has control over.

The danger comes into play when the cycle is broken in some way, and there is a possibility that the stepfather reacts violently as his paradigm of control over the household is shattered. Perhaps somewhere along the road, the victim realizes that things are never going to change and that the love and trust and respect that the mother once thought was there no longer exists. They decide to leave permanently and even reach out to government agencies and other family members for support. They try to plan a quiet escape, but the stepfather finds out and immediately gets angry to the point of rage.

Many tragic endings have followed such a scenario in real life, and it highlights the need for support in the area of domestic abuse victims who are trying to get out of a dangerous and toxic environment at home.

Another set of circumstances where the parent might exercise emotional manipulation is in the case of an absent parent who later comes back to ask for support from an adult child. Even when a parent is absent, there is a bond and desire for connection with the child in most cases, which might drive them to find the parent later in life to try to rekindle the relationship. In another scenario, the child is strong enough to accept that even though this person is family, they have not earned the love and respect that would have been afforded had they actually functioned like a parent in the home. When an estranged parent comes to a point in their lives when they really don't see any other means of support other than their children, things can get awkward and heartbreaking really fast.

After that initial approach, the parent usually hides the fact that they need help and pretends that the meeting is all about wanting to apologize and reintroduce himself into the child's life. He must then watch the child's response and play according to how open and willing he is to give in and let his father talk. If there is any degree of desire for reconnection or existing love even after having been abandoned, then the father might be able to latch onto this and go along with the idea that they are forming a relationship that both had missed out on while the child was growing up. This is another form of toxic emotional manipulation,

which plays on a child's love for his parents, even when they are not the best parents in the world. Just like the example above where the parents give in to a son who is increasingly absent and becoming distant in their lives, there is a very strong unconditional love that is present in many families, which can be very difficult to overcome in toxic and manipulative situations. The abuser will milk this tendency for all it's worth where their needs or desires are desperate, while the victims desperately cling to the possibility that they can change things for the better each time they are manipulated into helping out the abuser in some way.

Chapter 10: Defenses Against Brainwashing

Brainwashing is a manipulation technique in which the abuser completely alters a victim's frame of mind concerning some aspects involved with the abuser's desire or intent for the victim. To illustrate, we will look more deeply at the example of the cult, which manages to grow in number through the use of recruiters and which maintains support through the use of brainwashing, which manifests in different ways and strategies.

How Is Brainwashing Accomplished?

There is an antiquated idea of what brainwashing is that is common among people who have, thankfully, never been subject to such a practice. Most people refer immediately to science fiction movies or something like that to reference what they think they know about brainwashing. Contrary to some popular beliefs, brainwashing does not involve taking over another person's brain and turning them into some kind of robot. The victim does not completely involuntarily take action according to the abuser's wishes; their minds are rather conditioned over time to think a certain way based on false paradigms that are constructed and made believable by the abuser.

Others might confuse brainwashing and hypnotism, which is a completely different practice involving different intended outcomes. The hypnotist is usually a person who practices the therapy on someone who is struggling with some kind of mental ailment, such as PTSD, and is repressing memory in order to avoid addressing the issues deep inside. The hypnotist's job is to help the victim root out these repressed memories so that they can be processed in a healthy way so the victim can continue to develop emotionally instead of remaining stunted and stuck in a place without ever moving forward with their lives. Brainwashing techniques are utilized for the sake of the abuser's intents and not necessarily the victim's desire. It is a directly manipulative tactic that does not really have the victim's well-being at heart, though it can be made to look like an altruistic effort. Let's look at how something like this might play out in the cult example.

Marsha is a middle-aged woman who has worked in a factory for almost all of her working life. She has grown quite skilled in what she does, and she is minimally satisfied with the state of affairs at home, where she works alongside a husband raising their daughter, who is 8 years old. She feels empty somehow and isn't quite sure what is wrong with her, but she attempts to look for answers through an online site called MeetUp, where she might find some like-minded women who are in similar circumstances as her. She has never been a religious person, but she is also open-minded about the philosophies of the world and has always had a curious mind that loves to learn about new ideas. She finds a group of women online who are advertised as a kind of social group where they get together regularly to talk and discuss things about their lives in a safe environment where no one is judged for what they share. Marsha thinks about the idea for a while before sending an email to the leader of the group for more information about the group. The first step toward an impending brainwashing attempt follows in the form of a return email from the leader. Let us call her Sam.

Sam's message is relayed in a way that oozes with warmth and understanding for why Marsha has reached out. She makes the interaction sound effortless and puts herself on the same level as Marsha, sharing that she also has a young child and was looking for some kind of social support in the form of other similar women who might understand her situation. She also says she understands the feeling of wanting something more in her life but being unsure of what exactly that something might be. She has known, met, and talked with many women who were in this boat and then strongly encourages Marsha to consider coming to one of their gatherings. The meetings themselves are explained to be low-pressure and purely social and fun in nature. There is no obligation to share any more details about one's life than she feels comfortable with. It's not really a support group or a therapy group; it's just that a lot of women have developed close relationships within the group to the point where they feel comfortable sharing things about their lives in order to get helpful feedback. Sam relays to Marsha all about how she first started the group and how she has met such wonderful women in the process. She keeps the tone in the email both light and passionate so as not to scare Marsha away with a level of intimacy but to also draw her in with the prospect of hanging out with some fun women who are refusing to let the weight of life keep them down. Sam ends the email with a friendly remark and says that she hopes to hear from Marsha soon. She includes the details for their next meeting.

After reading this email, Marsha immediately feels a sense of excitement about the prospect and immediately has a conversation with her husband to see how he might feel about it. Marsha describes the group as a bunch of women who get together and socialize and talk about their lives. It is women-only, and he turns his brow up a bit at that remark but soon decides that it seems like a harmless undertaking and encourages his wife to try a meeting or two if that is what she wants to do. He is happy that she is excited about trying this out, as he has also picked up on the fact that she hasn't been completely happy or seemed fulfilled personally for a while. So, Marsha plans to go to the next meeting.

The meeting is held at one of the members' homes, and the place feels quite cozy and inviting as Marsha enters. There are a few fragrant candles around, and as she moves into the room, every one of the women there comes forward and introduces herself with a smile. Marsha immediately felt at home and welcomed. She is offered refreshments and then invited to sit down and speak with a couple of women in the living room. There are a few different conversations evolving at once instead of one big discussion, which helps Marsha feel at ease as she was worried about being asked to speak in front of a large group. Instead, she begins conversing with a small group of three other women who listen intently as Marsha introduces herself and what's going on in her life. She already feels much more at ease as she is being listened to. The conversation continues, and the other women also talk about their lives and open themselves up in terms of vulnerability as they describe some things that they are struggling with personally. Marsha is struck by how they feel comfortable talking about such personal things with these women, but it also makes her feel like these women could become close friends in whom she could confide. She offers her own insights and suggestions as each of the ladies speak, and she begins to divulge details about her own life and her own

sense of missing something important and meaningful.

In this first meeting, there will not be any overt mention of the gathering's hidden intentions in the situation where there are any. The goal for an initial meeting is to make the potential initiate feel as safe and secure as possible. They want to surround her with warmth and make her feel like she can trust these women who only have her best interests at heart. This essential step works to encourage the victim to let her guard down and to feel like she can reveal areas of vulnerability, which will be the cult's secret weapon.

Once the women know Marsha's areas of vulnerability, they can home in on that factor as a way to gradually convince her that they can help and bring her fulfillment and happiness in all the ways she is looking for. After this initial meeting, she is likely to come back and then continue to come as something she looks forward to each week. As the meetings continue, she will start to think of these women as friends, as they also work toward convincing Marsha that they have answers to her problems. At some point, when the timing is right, the women might introduce one of the cult's covert practices, which involves goings-on that are quite foreign to her. But because of her developed relationship and sense of trust between the women, as well as her natural curiosity, Marsh agrees to attend and watch a ritual where the women turn their attention to some kind of deity at work, taking care of their souls and granting desires in exchange for services. Now, obviously, this example is a little out there, but the focus here is on the gradual manipulation process which works to enfold a victim into a circle of warmth where things they would never have considered involving themselves in before becoming more and more possible because of the prior conditioning received from the women. After all, at this point, she is receiving information and suggestions from people she considers friends, and with that comes a level of trust and suspension of disbelief for their sake.

The ritual is explained in terms that are not too intimidating, and the terms are often less dramatic than how other people would define these proceedings. The word cult is never used, for example, and the words used to describe everything are soft, if not entirely inaccurate. This is slowly to let Marsha get used to the idea of what is happening without flipping a switch that starts to signal red flags. The emphasis is put on the fact that these proceedings have helped the women in the group solve their problems and find solace and peace and fulfillment—things that Marsha has also been looking for in her life. The very fact that these promises seem to be targeted directly toward her makes her feel as if she has fallen into the hands of destiny, and it has finally let her find what she has been looking for. When people's deepest desires and wants are revealed, and something manifests a promise of fulfillment in return, people are likely to engage in practices and belief systems that would have seemed outlandish and ridiculous in the past. But a cult never underestimates human desire for spiritual fulfillment and peace, so they have learned how to tap into the darkest corners of another person's mind in order to root out those hidden desires and needs. At his point, Marsha is all but initiated and fully involved in the cult's way of life and belief systems.

How to Avoid Brainwashing?

Knowing we are all human beings and susceptible to manipulation that targets emotions, desires, and other areas where people are generally quite vulnerable, how can you defend yourself against someone who is trying to use these against you in a brainwashing attempt? The advice here follows the advice given in the previous chapters, where potential manipulation is involved. You must maintain awareness in all situations and consider the possibility that the people you are talking to are not who they say they are. The golden rule in situations like this is the following: If it seems too good to be true, then it probably is.

Similar to a financial scheme in which someone tricks others into investing in false promises or nonexistent entities, the person or 'business' is convinced as something where they can make a whole lot of money for very little time, effort, and personal risk. This happens a lot of the time. It is quite impossible, and people should be aware of the schemes at work in the real world, which prey on people's simple desires for money and to get it the easy way. On a deeper level, there are those who know that they can manipulate their way into someone's heart and circle of trust by promising quick fixes for the things which plague many human beings. These are things that have to do with deep spiritual

fulfillment or finding peace or meaning in daily life, which sometimes seems like a road full of emptiness, especially when there are hardships to work through. Be aware of those deepest vulnerabilities that you harbor in yourself, and work to find your own way to fulfillment and satisfaction or meaning. Do not put yourself in other human beings where this deepest desire is concerned because this is the gateway for emotional manipulation and brainwashing according to another person or group's will. Remember that the most important things in life are worked for and sought after for a long period of time and only with the help of those you love, trust, and respect based on your own choosing and experience with them. Do not let people, who promise answers to all your problems, come into your life because quick fixes just don't exist. Be aware of the ulterior motives that might exist. Do not reveal personal information that might be used against you, but instead, make others prove themselves trustworthy through tests of time and trial.

Now that you know the general workings behind brainwashing techniques keep in mind that genuine relationships happen naturally and not according to a timeline. In the example above, Marsha fell into a trap based on her own feelings and was able to fall right in line according to a very short timeline where she should have been developing a meaningful relationship with these women with whom she chose to share personal information and issues. A large factor in this downfall was an element of group pressure where everyone around her was

acting a certain way, and this made her feel like she should be acting in the same way, too. And this involved divulging her deepest struggles. If something similar feels like having an impression on you and your behavior, it is best to remove yourself from the situation so that you have time to think clearly about what's going on. Anytime you feel doubt about a new interaction and acquaintance, let the people already in your life, whom you love and trust, help you work through what you truly feel regarding that budding relationship. Someone else might be able to pinpoint red flags when you are too distracted to notice them yourself.

Chapter 11: Neuro-Linguistic Programming

What Is NLP?

Neuro-linguistic programming is an area of research as well as a practice that involves the way we think as human beings in conjunction with language. Even if you're not familiar with the term, most readers will be familiar with some common mindfulness strategies which employ the elements of the NLP techniques, such as the law of attraction, cognitive behavioral therapy, and the way we talk ourselves through times of anxiety or nervousness. Think of the professor who is getting ready to go out in front of a large classroom of college students for the first time and how she might feel very nervous. To calm herself down, she walks through in her mind how she has been preparing for years, that she is completely prepared, and there is nothing to worry about, etc. All of the scenarios have the potential to encourage a change in mindset to serve the individual in specific scenarios. The process follows as the person recognizes the situation and how his brain automatically responds, then engages a strategy using language and repetition to alter how the brain will process and respond to the given situation the individual is trying to overcome.

The basis of this research involves how the brain processes and responds to information on a regular basis and the paradigms the mind forms as a response to this experience over time. First, it's important to gain an understanding of what we're talking about when we talk about how the brain processes information.

Every day, we are all inundated with information coming into our brains through our senses. This information comes in many forms, and when the brain gets overloaded with information to the point where it has to start picking and choosing what and when to process, we call this information overload. Information overload occurs all the time when we are simply surrounded by too much in the way of stimuli, and the brain simply can't process everything that is coming in. In order to make sense of the world, human beings have developed a process for categorization and prioritizing according to what we consciously and subconsciously deem as more of a priority than other kinds of information. But the brain can actually work against us in some respects when it begins to process information out of habits that have developed from negative experiences. For example, phobias can be formed based on just a single experience that occurred and made a dramatic impression on the one having the experience. Let us say a child accidentally walks straight into a spider web and immediately feels spiders crawling on his skin. The boy grows up to harbor an intense fear and anxiety around spiders, and this anxiety awakens each time he is confronted with a spider. The sensitivity could be so extreme that even the mention of spiders in conversation prompts a neurologic response, and the subject begins to feel a panic attack. His mind begins tricking him into thinking there is a spider crawling on him. These processes are our body's ways of protecting us from future harm based on past experiences, but sometimes, this process hinders us from moving forward or getting past things that are not actually real threats to our well-being. The mind and body mean well, but the subject needs to somehow alter the way in which his brain is processing this particular piece of information so that the fear and anxiety that are triggered do not hold him back from living his life with confidence. Perhaps he wants to go on a backpacking trip that will involve hiking through wooded areas, but his anxiety and spider phobia keep

getting in the way, so he is finding it difficult to say yes to the excursion, even though he really wants to do it. The individual might be able to benefit from NLP research and tactics as a way to reprogram his mind to process this particular information differently in a way that will help him instead of hold him back.

The good news in this scenario is that research in the past few decades have discovered an innate malleability and plasticity, which are inherent in the human brain. This means that we can teach our brains to react differently if we practice a kind of cognitive re-programming in the moment. Over time and with repetition, the brain will learn to react with complacency and confidence rather than fear and anxiety, and it relearns through retraining what the subject wants to happen in those moments. The subject in this scenario might first come to terms with the idea that the fear itself is irrational and simply a product of past childhood experiences. When faced with this anxiety, perhaps through showing pictures of spiders to him, the subject will then devise some sort of monologue to go along with the experience. The monologue might entail that this challenge is about preparation instead of fear and that the anxiety is a step toward understanding instead of anticipation of danger. The information is being received the same way mechanically, but we are rewriting the story we tell ourselves through the brain's understanding and reactions. The subject might come up with a certain behavior or mental command, which will redirect the anxiety and change it into something else before the feeling gets out of hand. With time and practice, the stimulus of the spider will trigger the conditioned responses that the brain has been trained to turn to in this specific situation, thus eradicating the anxiety and fear that had once accompanied the stimulus.

Let us look at another example. Many people suffer with anxiety in a generalized way, which makes the anxiety rise at sometimes unpredictable times throughout the day, and these episodes are often accompanied by panic attacks. Panic attacks can be quite debilitating, first as the experience itself is quite uncomfortable, but also because the subject learns to be anxious about the potential of an impending anxiety attack, compounding its effect and impact on a day-to-day basis.

There are different treatments available for this kind of ailment, and rewiring the brain's response to life's unpredictable situations can be helpful in this process of alleviating as much anxiety as possible on a regular basis. The rewiring happens as the subject practices a consistent application of a narrative that is different from the one which encourages fear and doubt. For example, a subject might  teach herself to acknowledge anxiety as her body's way of readying herself for an experience as it becomes hyper-aware of everything in her surroundings. As this is supported and backed up over time and with repetition, the subject might then add in additional ways of processing information as the narrative moves along. It is a kind of misdirection that enables the subject to move in a different direction than the one that has been developed as a habit based on events and past negative experiences. The subject should work to replace these negative experiences with the positive ones in which the body's anxiety responses help bring awareness to a situation, helping the subject navigate the scenario successfully. The brain is working alongside the conscious self to improve upon a behavior in response to certain information or stimuli, and that is neuro-linguistic programming.

How is NLP Used in a Manipulation Scheme?

So how can NLP be used against a subject as part of some manipulation scheme employing dark psychology? Well, if we all know individually that we can have an impact on ourselves through language and redirecting the brain, those who have some knowledge in psychology also realize the significance of this phenomenon. The impact of language and the accumulation of that language coming from several different individuals can have a huge impact on the mindset of the target. This is why phenomena like peer pressure and groupthink have been established as clear indications of the social aspect of human beings' process of forming opinions and ideas about others and their experiences. Groupthink is the phenomenon where a group of people working together might be influenced by each other to a large degree in a way that shuts down the creativity and innovation that comes from individual thought processing. An individual is pulled into the group's opinions and thought processes instead of feeling the freedom to innovate and come up with individual creative ideas because of a mix of psychological factors, such as peer pressure and not wanting to stick out or be different from the crowd. As the ideas fly around in the form of words and shared thoughts, this process becomes solidified as the brain does not make room for anything other than the information being thrown at it by other people. In this way, the potential for an innovative idea that comes from a single creative mind might be squashed under the weight of the collective thought and creation process, leading to lots of missed opportunities.

A similar phenomenon occurs when a single target is focused by those aiming to utilize NLP in order to sway the target's mind in a particular direction. The intentions and motivations behind these actions might vary from simply wanting to form a negative opinion of someone else in the target to trying to cause the target to take a harmful action toward another target. Factors such as being in a position of authority or power can have an added impact in these endeavors, and they are not always conscious endeavors on the part of the manipulators. A prime example is the high school environment.

Most of us probably remember the days when what the popular kids said about  you had a bit of impact on how other peers thought about you. If you were one of those popular kids, then you might remember how your opinions and statements about other people tended to carry a lot more weight than the words of someone who was less popular. It doesn't even matter how much evidence there was to support the claims or opinions of people; it was simply a matter of disseminating information mixed with some other influential factor, in this case, popularity. When a person with some kind of influential power speaks, people are more willing and primed to listen and form opinions in line with what they are hearing. And the more this gets reinforced, the stronger the influential factor. Gossip can be a strong manipulation tool in that people tend to be drawn toward many aspects of gossip. Gossip between peers within some kind of organization structure, like high school, makes those involved feel like they are included in something bigger than themselves, while the targets are not. It is a form of pushing others down while you boost yourself up. Sometimes, especially as a teenager, this can feel like a survival mechanism that is just absolutely necessary to your existence in school. No one wants to be the odd one out, or the one everyone is gossiping about. Therefore, it pays to be part of the gossip itself while it is targeting someone else. If it is hurting someone else, that means it's not hurting you. Now, these things might not be the conscious flow of thought coming from your average teenager, but there are psychological underpinnings to all high school behavior that do not have to be consciously enacted to be effective and predictable.

One of the best practices to avoid falling into these psychological traps of influence is simply not to believe everyone you hear, especially if it is gossip! Gossip can be utilized for all the wrong reasons, and, at the end of the day, it doesn't really matter if what you are hearing is wrong or right. The reality is that you are letting secondary sources of information guide your thoughts and opinions about someone you may have never even talked to before. Don't let the allure of being included in the group draw you down in this regard. In other words, it is wise not to be drawn to others' level, especially if doing so means that you are ganging up on another human being. Think about how this would make you feel yourself; if several people started thinking erroneous things about you and developed a negative opinion without any evidence that those rumors are warranted. This is not a position you would ever want to be in, so do not inflict this position on others. A person must always be aware of the vulnerabilities and fallacies present in the nature of being human and the capacity to make mistakes and make inappropriate and inaccurate judgments toward others. One of the consistent pieces of advice appearing throughout this book is to simply be aware that you are not immune to subconscious influence. No one is too smart to be manipulated, and those who think they are, make themselves prime targets for manipulation and emotional abuse. Those who think they are the most infallible often become the weakest link when it comes to psychological practices to inflict harm simply because they do not understand the fallible nature of their minds and, therefore, never acknowledge that they need to safeguard themselves against manipulators. NLP, in the form of flattery through words, can have a huge impact on someone whose ego is already quite large. Placing yourself above others in your mind can be a quick way to a long fall, and often the victim in this scenario will not realize the truth until it is too late and they are too far down the rabbit hole.

Chapter 12: Covert Mind Control

The idea of covert mind control is wrapped in lots of different packages and sold on a variety of levels for different reasons. For example, you might see lots of online ads or videos claiming to be able to teach you to hypnotize your wife or control another person's behavior to your own ends. This type of targeted advertising might show up in social media or on websites and specifically targets those who are amateurs to the world of "mind control." They sell them the concept that in a short amount of time, you learn a few specific techniques,

develop the skills, and accomplish whatever you want.

The irony here is that this type of targeted marketing is a form of covert mind control and follows the lines of many age-old marketing and selling techniques, which are still effective today. This follows because the human being's brain and how it thinks is essentially the same, though the environment and the mode of information and how it is spread has changed drastically.

The Subliminal Message Experiment

Covert mind control is a facet of dark psychology, which aspires to direct a person's actions based on subconscious commands that are planted without the targets knowing about it. The idea of hypnosis and what was called "subliminal" messaging became popular in the 70s when an interesting experiment took place with the intention of luring out an evasive killer on the loose. Here's how the experiment went down.

Law enforcement teamed up with a TV news network to broadcast a subliminal message to all who happened to be watching the show. While the reporters discussed the crimes of the killer and the details surrounding their occurrences, a very brief slide would show up on the screen for just a fraction of a second, far too fast for anyone to actually make out what it was in real time. It looked like just a blip on the screen, and most people would simply dismiss it shortly afterward. But the "blip" was actually a visual image, which contained what law enforcement hoped would be a cue that the killer would see and follow due to the subconscious embedding of a command. The message itself was quite simple. It was a command to contact law enforcement, and it contained a visual cue in the form of a pair of eyeglasses similar to a pair found at the killer's latest crime scene. At the time, it was thought that the killer kept up with the news broadcasts about his crimes and that he would surely be tuning in to this particular show. They also believed that there was a chance that subliminal messaging could be effective enough to actually get the killer to pick up the phone or perhaps walk into the station and turn himself in. The notion is quite comical nowadays, and needless to say, the tactic did not work. But there was a lot going on in those days in the realm of psychology research and practices such as profiling to help law enforcement and detectives hunt down perpetrators and killers, the likes of which the country had never seen before. The 70s were a time when the term serial killer was just beginning to be included in the language of detectives working multiple crime scenes, where the same person seemed to be making his attacks following a consistent "M.O." or modus operandi, with short breaks of varying lengths in between killings. The modus operandi referred to the exact way in which the killer carried out his murders.

The subliminal messaging tactic did not work, but the research on human psychology and mind control never ceased to continue and garner support and dedicated researchers along the way.

Art of Embedded Commands

Another form of covert mind control in practice today is the art of embedded commands. There are some similarities between the theory behind embedded commands and subliminal messaging in that the idea is to communicate with the subconscious without the subconscious mind really knowing what's going on. The same principle has been applied in the theory that says you can teach yourself things in your sleep by running certain messages through earphones worn by the subject during sleep. This experiment has been run many times for a variety of different purposes. Some people believe that a person can progress through a period of grief much more quickly through the use of such sleep therapy, while others swear that their knowledge of a foreign language has been drastically improved through letting their subconscious minds listen to narratives in the foreign language while the subject is sleeping.

Embedded commands work similarly but are instead words hidden within a larger pool of words in a way that influences the listener without the listener necessarily realizing there is influence or commanding going on. This kind of "mind control" is practiced most often and most recognizably in sales and marketing, especially online marketing in today's digital world. Ads that follow this model of embedded messaging progress a lot like a specific argument in the mode of Aristotle's logos, as has been briefly discussed. The idea is to construct a series of statements that flow logically together and which lead the listener to end up at a point where the final argument seems like the only logical, rational conclusion to the series of arguments. These arguments are designed to feel intuitive and natural as if nothing in the world could replace the obvious truth unfolding before you in the form of the logical procession of statements leading to a given answer.

In a marketing ad, the flow usually goes something like this.

You need something, you want something, and you have to get something that you do not already have. This need can be anything from being prettier, fitter, happier, better at getting things done at work, smarter, more impressive, etc. The list can go on and on, according to any kind of product the marketer is trying to sell. The idea is to first inspire the viewer or reader or listener to realize a certain void in his/her life that needs to be filled. Most of the time, this need does not really objectively exist in the way the ad will try to convince you it does, and with urgency. Not only do you "need" whatever it is they tell you that you need, but you also need it immediately. Once the ad has you thinking about whatever it is you are lacking, they might employ another kind of tactic to throw in so that you are solidly trapped in this way of thinking that you need something. There are several ways an ad will accomplish this. Some might show other people who have bought the product who are obviously much happier than you because of it. Others will employ the use of someone famous to tell you that you're crazy if you don't buy into the idea that you need this product, etc. Others will entice the viewer or reader with images of the product itself in all its grandeur, usually a much-exaggerated depiction in terms of visual appeal. Think of the tasty hamburger images that often accompany fast food commercials. At this point, the ad has hooked you insofar as your interest. Next, they have to pitch their answer to your dilemma. In other words, "don't despair; we know you really need this thing. That's why we have this product for you m, and it will solve all of your problems!" From there, it is a matter of direct sales pitching that will utilize different combinations of tactics. Some will state that you only have a limited time to take advantage of an offer. This prompts the sense of urgency in the potential buyer that they have to act fast, thereby encouraging an impulse buy. Other ads will compare themselves to other competitors' prices and talk about how much better their products are than the competition, etc. All of this is designed with a specific process of covert mind control at work, which convinces the viewer or reader that they are making a rational decision when they decide to buy, even though the very idea of buying was implanted into their brains when they decided to read or watch the ad.

Often, we don't even get a say in whether or not we want to be exposed to such ads. This is especially true online when we are engaged in routine practices like scrolling through social media feeds. Our data is compiled and sold to companies who then can design very specific ads and images that will prompt our desire to buy things in a way that the marketers already know we are susceptible to.

Online data has become a very hot-button issue in recent years, and the arguments about the morality of online marketing and "fake news" in the form of ads on social media are particularly under fire, mainly for influencing people's behavior around political elections. These ads worked to target viewers' psychological responses to things that their data has told marketers and ad designers will work on specific individuals. The ads are often visually assaulting and are designed to trigger emotional responses that will then feed into the desired behavior targeted by the ad, such as, "vote for me," "the competition is a bad person," etc. While the viewer feels as if she is thinking and making decisions of her own volition, there is a level of covert mind control that has a lot more influence on our sensibilities than most are willing to admit. And again, this is where the main weaknesses are embedded.

Convince the public that they are making rational decisions while they are being manipulated, and you have a very powerful mechanism for effective dark psychology.

The same questions arise from the realization of these kinds of covert practices at work. How can we recognize when dark psychology is being used, and what can we do to protect ourselves?

Similar to other best practices outlined in this book, one of the best ways to avoid being taken advantage of in these contexts is to stay aware of the possibility that the information you are receiving is one-sided. Do your own research and find out if all the facts are being included in the stories you regularly see on your social media feeds. Also, make sure you know all facets to be known before formulating an opinion. Online marketing, especially in the political arena, has been noted to target those who seem more "on the fence" than others. These people make up lots of populations in swing states where the political vote has been known to swing back and forth by a relatively small margin at different points in time. During the 2016 election, it was these specific areas of interest in swing states which the Trump campaign ad team was able to target with social media ads attacking Hillary Clinton and inciting attitudes nearing that of hatred against her. These tactics have been cited in recent years as one of the leading factors contributing to Trump's presidential victory that year.

How to Protect Yourself From Covert Mind Control

When you read or take notice of these kinds of ads, whether they appear automatically in your social media feeds or on other news sites, it is important that you are taking everything in with a grain of salt and make sure to not let a single person or organization's opinion sway your own mind and opinion without a well-researched set of evidence and facts. Don't let your emotions be ignited ahead of your reasoning ability, such as with an image whose sole intent is to make you angry immediately and influence how you feel about a particular issue or news story. Remember that there are always going to be differing opinions and that it is up to you to get the full story and form your own opinions based on real evidence and how you feel personally in regards to your values, ethics, morals, etc. Put simply, don't believe everything you hear or read simply because it evokes a strong emotional response. This is a mind control tactic, and you should always be on guard when you are online and going through many news stories and information being thrown at you at a higher rate.

Another way to help guide you in your endeavor to safeguard your own mind and emotions is to have an open discussion with the people in your life whom you respect and trust. Get their points of view and see where they get their information, why they believe what they believe, etc. You may disagree with some things that they are saying, but it can help you get some perspective against getting your information and opinions from talking heads online. You might hear some interesting arguments put in a way that you had never heard before, and this might prompt you to see things in a different light or at least contemplate the different possibilities and points of view out there. This is very important in forming a well-educated set of beliefs and values. Don't even be afraid to expand your horizons and listen to others, especially those you disagree with. Get all the facts and respect that different people have and that this process should be safeguarded against dark psychology tactics.

Chapter 13: Recognizing Manipulators

In this chapter, we will list several tips for you to memorize and keep close by when you want to safeguard yourself against potentially manipulative people. It helps to have these tips memorized so that you teach your brain to automatically recognize them when these warning signs appear.

They Constantly Challenge You to Prove Yourself and Show Affection

When you are dealing with someone who is constantly asking you to prove how you feel about them, there is a possibility that there is a manipulation attempt at work. People trying to manipulate you will often keep you on your toes to the point where you feel guilty when you are not giving in to their demands. This can be emotionally draining because you feel guilty that the person does not realize the extent of your compassion or love you have for them but are also confused as to how you are not doing enough. This mixture of confusion, guilt, and mental exhaustion creates a perfect hunting ground for the emotional manipulator.

They Are Passive-Aggressive

The nature of the manipulator is to slide influence in under the radar. This nature contributes to their affinity for being passive-aggressive instead of direct, even when it is incredibly hurtful and founded in spite. At the heart of this behavior is a profound fear of losing control, and not being direct means that they are not facing the consequences of a direct confrontation.

They Use Gaslighting on You

As we've discussed in previous chapters, gaslighting is a toxic manipulation tactic that works to convince the victim that they cannot rely on their own recollections and sense of reason in arguments or other situations. The victim's sense of self-awareness and confidence in her own reality is completely broken down over a period of time. The practice of gaslighting is a huge indicator that this person is practicing manipulation. Be confident in yourself and what you believe happened. Don't let someone else convince you that they know better than you if you were the one with direct experience. If direct communication and addressing the situation does not work initially, the manipulator is unlikely to ever admit defeat in this regard, and it is best to remove yourself from their environment or vice versa.

They Use Humor as a Weapon Against You

Manipulators might go too far when it comes to turning a hurtful situation into something that was "just a joke." This works in their benefit if and when you choose to address it and explain that your feelings were hurt because they can come back and accuse you of being sensitive and unable to "take a joke." Don't fall for this tactic. If someone has hurt your feelings, joke or otherwise, it should be acknowledged or addressed because the pain itself is very real. It doesn't matter if it was supposed to be a joke or not.

They Are Always the Victim

People who are working as the manipulator in a relationship will often turn the "victim card" in an effort to redirect your anger and alleviate any sense of being in the wrong in the first place. This might manifest as a sudden switch from anger to sadness in the form of elephant tears and an apparent breaking down in front of you. The manipulator will quickly try to list all the ways in which she is not responsible for negative consequences and try to turn the blame around to be placed on the partner.

They Use Kindness as a Weapon

People who are out to get something from you often try to incite a feeling of obligation and a sense that you "owe" them through giving you things freely and treating you with excessive kindness and generosity. This way, the next time they need something from you, they can cite that one time they did something for you in the hopes that you will feel guilty and give in to their demands.

They Belittle Your Pain

A skilled manipulator will be able to belittle your pain by making your problems and issues out to be nothing significant. This is designed to make you feel like you should be stronger or able to handle things like everyone else, prompting feelings of guilt, shame, and especially inadequacy. The manipulator can use these feelings against you in different ways, such as making you more suggestible to their advice or to doing things "their way." They seem stronger than you because they do not have the same struggles and recognize your struggles as those with which only the weak have problems.

They Keep Their Cool to Magnify Your Own Emotions

When something stressful happens that gets you upset, one way for a manipulator to feel superior is not to react in the same way. Instead, they handle

themselves in a completely calm and cool manner. This way, they emphasize to themselves and anyone around that you are the one losing control, while they seem to be completely unbothered by the situation. They can then come at you with an accusation that you need to work on controlling your emotions.

Chapter 14: Manipulating Manipulators

Finally, this is something you can work on to completely derail someone who is trying to manipulate you—learn how to give them a taste of their own medicine. One of the most satisfying experiences in this arena would be to catch someone completely off guard while they are in the middle of a scheme that makes them feel superior to you.

Mirror the Manipulator

One way to pull this off is to practice the art of mirroring yourself in the context of a public gathering. Now that you know how a manipulator works, you can conduct an experiment when you feel that someone is trying to use flattery and mirroring to get on your good side. To do this, simply employ the personality of someone other than yourself. Perhaps you tell jokes with exaggerated enthusiasm or adopt a super serious affect. If the person who approaches you chooses to mirror these aspects, you will notice right away because of the jarring difference between the personality you've chosen and the personality being mirroring before you. At an integral moment in the conversation, switch gears to convey your own personality, and see how this person responds. If they are thrown off, the odds are, they were trying to mirror you, and now, they don't know what to do. If they are smart, they will realize what is happening and high-tail it away from you in embarrassment. It is likely this person won't be bothering you again.

Be Immune to the Manipulator's Charms

Another way to shut down a manipulator is simply to refuse to let them get under your skin. A manipulator trying to seduce you by charming you or get you angry to prompt an outburst, make you feel guilty, make you cry, or cave in are all tactics employed by the dark psychology user. You will be able to throw the frustration on their faces when they realize that their tactics are not going to work on you as you keep a straight face and a cool demeanor. Granted, this is easier said than done.

In order to enforce this kind of awareness and control over your emotions, you must first really get in touch with and address those areas of vulnerability you see in yourself. If you are someone who empathizes and cries easily when you see others in pain, it is important to be aware that this particular vulnerability can be taken advantage of in certain circumstances. If a complete stranger approaches you and starts right in on a sob story, then it would be wise to not give in with your emotions before you can verify its validity or weed out the purpose behind this person unloading this information onto you. If the context is inappropriate, then your senses should be telling you that this person might not have the most ethical intentions.

Be Aware of Your Emotions

The bottom line here is that the best way to undermine a manipulator and throw his own tactics to his face is to remain in control and fully aware of your own emotional state. Even if it means behaving in a way that seems rude or impolite, take a moment to really think about where this particular anxiety comes from. Do you genuinely feel that defending yourself and putting up an emotional guard in certain ways is inherently "rude," or did you just buy into that idea based on what other people tell you or convey to you? What is in your best interest? Let these arguments serve you through lines of reason and personal judgment before letting other people or society tell you what is and is not appropriate in social contexts. Don't ever fall for the feeling of obligation that may lead you into a situation where you feel uncomfortable. If you've been invited to a party full of strangers and something feels off, then leave. It's as simple as that. Don't fret about what your friend will think about you or what people will say. Your safety comes first.

A word of caution before getting overly defensive or confronting a dark psychology user is imperative here as we close this book. The very nature of a manipulator is that their emotions have some degree of volatility, and you can never know exactly how someone is going to react. Especially if you are in a situation where you are alone with the manipulator, think twice before throwing their tactics to their face. It might be wiser to play the game until you have a chance to call someone for help or get support from someone, including the police, in order to remove yourself from the situation. The scenarios will vary, and you could be in a public setting, like a party or club, and you simply wish to make it clear that you are not a good target for the manipulator's schemes. Use your common sense and judgment in these situations, and remember that even though it might make you feel good about yourself by exposing the manipulator, it is never worth putting yourself or others in danger.

Conclusion

Thank you for making it to the end of *Dark Psychology Secrets 2021: Defenses Against Covert Manipulation, Mind Control, NLP, Emotional Influence, Deception, and Brainwashing*. Let's hope it was informative and able to provide you with all of the tools you need to achieve your goals, whatever they may be.

You now have the knowledge and know-how you need to stay on guard throughout your day-to-day life against those who might seek to manipulate you. We encourage you to share what you've learned with others so that they might also benefit from what you've learned.

The modes of persuasion and different tactics used by manipulators are no longer a great mystery to you, as you can now recognize when the warning signs appear and how to remove yourself from the situation when you feel uncomfortable. You've learned that manipulation plays on many different emotions and that no two manipulators have the exact same intentions in mind. The defense inherent in learning all about manipulative techniques is finding out that the warning signs become obvious where, previously, you may not have recognized at all what might be happening. It is important to trust your instincts and not just go with the flow at all times for fear of sticking out or being the oddball. This impulse has led many unsuspecting victims into an impending tragedy, so don't let this happen to you. Stay near to those whom you truly know, love, trust, and respect, and guard these gifts when it comes to new relationships.

It is important that, although you stay on guard against potential manipulative techniques, you also do not fall into a dark place where you no longer engage with anyone outside your own home. Do not let the fear of having to confront a dark psychology user interfere with your life and your goals. There are lots of amazing people to meet and interact with, which will add so much value to your life. The key is to simply remain steadfast in what you require from another human being before you become willing to bestow on them the level of trust and love that you have for your friends and family who are in your life now.

Remember that a lot of support can be utilized through having honest and open communication with your friends and loved ones whom you trust. There is often a great deal of wisdom to be learned from talking to those who may have actually experienced what you are afraid to confront. Be aware of your own vulnerabilities, and don't be afraid to let these trusted individuals help you with whatever emotional weaknesses you see within yourself. By doing this, you are putting up a barrier between that which you know you are susceptible to and those who might try to get on your good side and exploit that particular emotional reaction. Take advice from those who are older or more experienced, and never take for granted that just because it hasn't happened to you yet, it never will. We are all potential victims. The difference between those who avoid catastrophe and those who don't is knowledge, along with mental preparation and awareness. You've made great strides toward strengthening all three of these safeguards, and we appreciate that you've chosen to begin your journey with this book. Share what you've learned, and continue working on yourself through whatever makes you feel happy, knowledgeable, and strong.

Finally, if you found this book useful in any way, a review is always appreciated!

www.ingramcontent.com/pod-product-compliance
Lightning Source LLC
Chambersburg PA
CBHW081344070526
44578CB00005B/720